The WORK of CHRIST

R. C. SPROUL

The WORK *of* CHRIST

WHAT THE EVENTS OF JESUS' LIFE MEAN FOR YOU

David C Cook®
transforming lives together

THE WORK OF CHRIST
Published by David C Cook
4050 Lee Vance View
Colorado Springs, CO 80918 U.S.A.

David C Cook Distribution Canada
55 Woodslee Avenue, Paris, Ontario, Canada N3L 3E5

David C Cook U.K., Kingsway Communications
Eastbourne, East Sussex BN23 6NT, England

The graphic circle C logo is a registered trademark of David C Cook.

The website addresses recommended throughout this book are offered as a
resource to you. These websites are not intended in any way to be or imply an
endorsement on the part of David C Cook, nor do we vouch for their content.

Unless otherwise noted, all Scripture quotations are taken from the New King
James Version®. Copyright © 1982 by Thomas Nelson, Inc. Used by permission.
All rights reserved. Scripture quotations marked ESV are taken from The Holy
Bible, English Standard Version® (ESV®), copyright © 2001 by Crossway, a
publishing ministry of Good News Publishers. Used by permission. All rights
reserved; KJV are taken from the King James Version of the Bible. (Public Domain.)

LCCN 2012934255
ISBN 978-0-7814-0726-7
eISBN 978-1-4347-0494-8

© 2012 R. C. Sproul
Published in association with the literary agency of Wolgemuth & Associates, Inc.

The Team: Alex Field, Nick Lee, Renada Arens, Karen Athen
Cover Design: Amy Konyndyk

Printed in the United States of America
First Edition 2012

1 2 3 4 5 6 7 8 9 10

031612

CONTENTS

PREFACE

ANY SIX-YEAR-OLD CHILD WHO has spent a few Lord's Day mornings in Sunday school is able to give an accurate answer to the question, "What did Jesus do for you?" Usually that child will say, "Jesus died on the cross for my sins." That's a true and profound statement, but it is only half of the matter.

If Jesus merely needed to die on the cross to save His people, He could have descended from heaven as a man on the morning of Good Friday, gone straight to Golgotha, died on the cross, risen, and left again. Our sin problem would be fixed. He did not need to be born to Mary in a stable, go through all the trials and tribulations of growing up in this fallen world, or endure the animosity of the Jewish leaders during His ministry.

However, Jesus did not live those thirty-three years for nothing.

In order for Him to qualify as our Redeemer, it was not enough for Him simply to go to the cross and be crucified. If Jesus had only paid for our sins, He would have succeeded only in taking us back to square one. We would no longer be guilty, but we still would have absolutely no righteousness to bring before God. So, our Redeemer needed not only to die, but also to live a life of perfect obedience. The righteousness that He manifested could then be transferred to all who put their trust in Him. Just as my sin is transferred to Him on the cross when I trust in Him, His righteousness is transferred to my account in the sight of God. So, when I stand before God on the judgment day, God is going to see Jesus and His righteousness, which will be my cover.

By His obedience, He redeemed His people for eternity.

It is important, then, that we not minimize the work of Christ throughout His life by focusing too narrowly on the work of Christ in His death. Thus, my purpose in this book is to give a brief overview of Christ's sojourn in this world, looking at the major events of both His life and His death to show that He fulfilled a lifelong mission. It is my prayer that this book will help you see that by His whole life our Lord wrought a complete salvation for His beloved people.

—R. C. Sproul
Sanford, Florida
October 2011

1

INCARNATION

IN THEOLOGY, WE MAKE a distinction between the person of Christ and the work of Christ for various reasons. But even though that distinction is important, we must never let it become a separation, because the person of Christ is intimately connected to His work. We understand His work largely from the perspective of the One who did the work. Conversely, the work of Jesus reveals a great deal about who He is. So, His person and His work may be distinguished but never separated.

In discussions of the work of Christ, many people believe that the natural place to begin is with His birth. However, the work of Christ began long before His birth. In fact, it began in eternity past, in what theologians call "the covenant of redemption." We encounter the word *covenant* frequently in the Bible. A covenant is a pact or agreement between two parties. There is the covenant of creation, the covenant of works, and the covenant of grace. As we read through the Scriptures, we see God making covenants with Noah, Abraham, and David, and later making the new covenant. However, many people are not familiar with the very first covenant, the covenant of redemption. That was not a covenant God made with human beings. Rather, the covenant of redemption was a pact forged in eternity among the three persons of the Godhead.

We distinguish the persons of the Godhead as the Father, the Son, and the Holy Spirit. When we examine the Old Testament record of creation, we see that the entire Trinity, the whole Godhead, was actively involved in bringing the universe into being. But not only creation was a Trinitarian work; so is redemption. In eternity before creation, the Father initiated the concept of redeeming the creation He knew would fall. He designed the plan of redemption. The Son was given the assignment to accomplish that redemption. The Holy Spirit was tasked with applying Christ's work of redemption to God's chosen people. It is vitally important that we understand that this division of responsibilities did not involve any imposition by the Father or a struggle within the Godhead itself. Rather, the Father, Son, and Spirit made an eternal agreement that is known as the covenant of redemption. Under this covenant, the Father sent the Son, and the Son was absolutely delighted to carry out the mission the Father gave Him.

The Apostle Paul sketched out the scope of Jesus' incarnation when he wrote, "Therefore He says: 'When He ascended on high, He led captivity captive, and gave gifts to men.' (Now this, 'He ascended'—what does it mean but that He also first descended into the lower parts of the earth? He who descended is also the One who ascended far above all the heavens, that He might fill all things)" (Eph. 4:8–10). So, the ministry of Jesus, which was crowned by His ascension to glory for His coronation as Lord of creation, began with His descent. He left His home in glory with the Father and the Spirit, and He came to this world by way of incarnation.

Likewise, at the opening of his epistle to the Romans, Paul identified himself as an Apostle called of God and set apart for the gospel of God, which, he said, was "promised before through His prophets in the Holy Scriptures, concerning His Son Jesus Christ our Lord, who was born of the seed of David according to the flesh" (1:2–3). Thus, Paul began his great exposition of the gospel and the work of Christ with a reference to Jesus being born as a descendant of David. This reference to Jesus' birth brings us immediately to the concept of incarnation.

THE BIRTH OF THE INCARNATE ONE

That which is significant about the birth of Christ, that which we celebrate at Christmas, is not so much the birth as the incarnation of God Himself. An incarnation is a coming in the flesh. In the prologue of his gospel, John first distinguished between the Word and God: "In the beginning was the Word, and the Word was with God" (1:1a). Then, in the very next breath, he said that They are the same: "The Word was God" (v. 1b). Finally, at the end of the prologue, he wrote, "And the Word became flesh and dwelt among us" (v. 14a). In this "incarnation," God did not suddenly undergo a metamorphosis into a man, so that the divine nature essentially passed out of existence or took on a new form. The incarnation was not so much a subtraction as it was an addition; the eternal second person of the Trinity took on Himself a human nature and joined His divine nature to that human nature for the purpose of redemption.

Paul had some very important things to say about the incarnation in his letter to the Philippians:

> Let this mind be in you which was also in Christ Jesus, who, being in the form of God, did not consider it robbery to be equal with God, but made Himself of no reputation, taking the form of a bondservant, and coming in the likeness of men. And being found in appearance as a man, He humbled Himself and became obedient to the point of death, even the death of the cross. Therefore God also has highly exalted Him and given Him the name which is above every name, that at the name of Jesus every knee should bow, of those in heaven, and of those on earth, and of those under the earth, and that every tongue should confess that Jesus Christ is Lord, to the glory of God the Father. (2:5–11)

This passage, which is a celebration of the incarnation of Christ, is known as the Kenotic Hymn. It is probable that the Apostle did not compose this passage while he was writing the letter to the Philippians, but that he made use of a hymn Christians were singing at the time. It is called the Kenotic Hymn because of a prominent Greek word that is found within this passage, *kenosis,* which literally means "an emptying." The image of emptying gives us an idea of the transition Jesus underwent by leaving His exalted state in heaven and becoming incarnate as a man in this world.

In the life of Jesus, we see a very distinct pattern of humiliation and exaltation. He began in exaltation in the glory of heaven, but He condescended to join us in our earthly existence in order to redeem us. By entering into human flesh, He underwent a profound humiliation. Throughout His lifetime, the humiliation became deeper and darker, finally reaching its nadir in the cross. After His crucifixion and death, the pattern changed, and He began to be exalted once more, beginning with His burial in the tomb of a wealthy man and culminating with His ascension to glory.

The pattern is not always consistent. Several years ago, I wrote a book titled *The Glory of Christ* because I was fascinated at the way in which, during Jesus' earthly life, when His eternal identity was shrouded during His incarnation, bursts of glory occasionally broke through, as if the incarnation was incapable of totally submerging His glory. We see it, for example, in Luke's account of the birth of Jesus. Luke tells us of the arduous journey that Mary and Joseph took in order to be registered in Bethlehem. When they got there, there was no room in the inn, so Jesus was born in the utter humiliation of a stable, wrapped in swaddling cloths, and laid in a manger. But even while we have this picture of humiliation, in the fields outside Bethlehem, the glory of God burst through, and the angelic chorus began to sing, "Glory to God in the highest, and on earth peace, goodwill toward men!" (Luke 2:14). That is just one example showing that Jesus' humiliation was not linear. Nevertheless, the basic pattern is one of humiliation to exaltation.

AN EXAMPLE TO EMULATE

I think it is important for us to note that Paul's purpose in the Kenotic Hymn was to show us how Jesus humbled Himself so that we might emulate Him. That is why Paul began by saying, "Let this mind be in you which was also in Christ Jesus" (Phil. 2:5). Elsewhere, the Apostle told us we must be willing to identify with the humiliation of Jesus if we hope to experience His exaltation (Rom. 8:17). Even our baptism displays humiliation and exaltation; in baptism, we are marked with the death of Jesus, but we also are marked with His resurrection.

Paul asserted that Christ, "being in the form of God, did not consider it robbery to be equal with God" (Phil. 2:6). That's strange language. Other translators say that Jesus did not consider equality with God a thing to be grasped. In other words, Jesus did not regard the glory that He enjoyed with the Father and the Spirit from all eternity as something to be guarded jealously and held tenaciously. Rather, He was willing to lay it aside. He was willing to empty Himself and make Himself "of no reputation" (v. 7a).

In the nineteenth century, liberal scholars propounded the kenotic theory of the incarnation, which declared that when Jesus came to this earth, He laid aside His divine attributes. Thus, the God-man no longer had the divine attributes of omniscience, omnipotence, and all the rest. Of course, this theory was a denial of the very nature of God, who is immutable. Even in the incarnation, the divine nature did not lose its divine attributes. Jesus did not communicate His divine attributes to His human side. He did not deify His human nature. The union between the divine and the human natures of Jesus is mysterious, but His human nature is truly human. That means it is not omniscient. It is not omnipotent. It is none of those things. At the same time, His divine nature remains fully and completely divine. A. E. Biedermann said that "only one who has himself suffered a kenosis of his understanding can possibly accord [kenotic theories] welcome."[1] In other words, these theologians had emptied themselves of their common sense.

In truth, Jesus emptied Himself of His glory, privilege, and exaltation. In the incarnation, He made Himself of no reputation. He allowed His divine, exalted standing to be subjected to human hostility, criticism, and even denial. He took the form of a bondservant and came in the likeness of a man (v. 7b). It is amazing enough that Jesus came as a man, but He also came as a slave. He came in a station that carried no exaltation or dignity at all, only indignity. In that state, "He humbled Himself and became obedient to the point of death, even the death of the cross" (v. 8).

FROM HUMILIATION TO EXALTATION

The words that follow this brief summary of the humiliation of Jesus in the incarnation are vitally important to us. Paul wrote, "Therefore God also has highly exalted Him and given Him the name which is above every name" (v. 9). In the upper room on the night before His execution, when Jesus prayed His High Priestly Prayer, one of His requests was that the Father would restore to Him the glory that They had together from the beginning. He said, "I have finished the work which You have given Me to do. And now, O Father, glorify Me together with Yourself, with the glory which I had with You before the world was" (John 17:4–5). The Father did exactly as Jesus asked at the completion of His work. There came an end to His indignity, to the humiliation that started so starkly with His birth.

The New Testament's names and titles for Jesus make for a rich and inspiring study. But what is the name that God has given Jesus, the name that is above every name? It often happens that Christians who read this passage assume that the name that is above every name is the name Jesus. But Paul had a different name in mind. He went on to say that God has exalted Christ and given Him the name above every name, "that at the name of Jesus every knee should bow, of those in heaven, and of those on earth, and of those under the earth, and that every tongue should confess that Jesus Christ is Lord, to the glory of God the Father" (Phil. 2:10–11). The name that is above every name is the title that belongs only to God, *Adonai* ("Lord"), which refers to God as the sovereign one. Because of Jesus' perfect obedience in the role of a slave, God moved heaven and earth to exalt His Son, and He gave Him the name that is above every name, so that when we hear the name of Jesus, our impulse should be to fall on our knees and confess that He is Lord to the glory of God the Father. When we do so, when we exalt Christ in this way, we also exalt the Father.

So, it comes full circle: first exaltation, then humiliation, and finally back to exaltation. Christ was not simply given the task of coming to die on Good Friday. He was called to live a lifetime of humiliation. That was the mission that He agreed to perform with the Father and the Spirit from all eternity.

CHAPTER 1

STUDY GUIDE

INTRODUCTION

So often, we think of the work of Christ as something that began when He was baptized in the Jordan River around the age of thirty. In reality, however, the work of Christ began in eternity past in the covenant of redemption. In this chapter, Dr. R. C. Sproul explains how the humiliation of Christ in His incarnation and crucifixion and the exaltation of Christ in His resurrection and ascension are both grounded in the eternal covenant among the persons of the Trinity.

LEARNING OBJECTIVES

1. To be able to state the relation of each of the persons of the Trinity to the covenant of redemption.
2. To be able to summarize the pattern of humiliation and exaltation in the work of Christ.

QUOTATIONS

> Let this mind be in you which was also in Christ Jesus, who, being in the form of God, did not consider it robbery to be equal with God, but made Himself of no reputation, taking the form of a bondservant, and coming in the likeness of men. And being found in appearance as a man, He humbled Himself and became obedient to the point of death, even the death of the cross. Therefore God also has highly exalted Him and given Him the name which is above every name, that at the name of Jesus every knee should bow, of those in heaven, and of those on earth, and of those under the earth, and that every tongue should confess that Jesus Christ is Lord, to the glory of God the Father.
>
> —Philippians 2:5–11

The pact of salvation makes known to us the relationships and life of the three persons in the Divine
Being as a covenantal life, a life of consummate
self-consciousness and freedom. Here, within the
Divine Being, the covenant flourishes to the full....
The greatest freedom and the most perfect agreement
coincide. The work of salvation is an undertaking of
three persons in which all cooperate and each per-
forms a special task.

—Herman Bavinck, *Reformed Dogmatics: Sin and
Salvation in Christ*

OUTLINE

I. Introduction

    A. In theology, we make a distinction between the person
of Christ and the work of Christ.

    B. Although the distinction is important, we must never let
it become a separation.

    C. We understand the work in light of the person doing the
work, and the work itself reveals a great deal about the
person.

II. The Covenant of Redemption

A. The work of Christ began in eternity past in the "covenant of redemption."

B. Although most Christians are familiar with the Abrahamic covenant, the Mosaic covenant, the Davidic covenant, and so on, not as many are familiar with the covenant of redemption.

C. The covenant of redemption refers to a pact or an agreement that takes place in eternity within the Godhead.

D. Not only is creation a Trinitarian work; redemption is a Trinitarian work.

E. The Father designed the plan of redemption.

F. The Son was assigned to accomplish that redemption.

G. The Holy Spirit is tasked with applying that redemption to us.

III. The Incarnation

A. During His earthly ministry, Jesus said, "No one has ascended to heaven but He who came down from heaven" (John 3:13).

B. Jesus' ministry in this world began with His descent.

C. Jesus was born of the seed of David according to the flesh.

D. In His birth we have the incarnation of God Himself.

E. The gospel of John tells us that the Word became flesh and dwelt among us (John 1:14).

F. In this "incarnation," God did not undergo metamorphosis into a man.

G. The incarnation was not so much a subtraction as an addition.

H. The eternal second person of the Trinity took upon Himself a human nature for the purpose of redemption.

IV. The Pattern of Humiliation and Exaltation

A. The Apostle Paul, in his letter to the Philippians, wrote: "Let this mind be in you which was also in Christ Jesus, who, being in the form of God, did not consider it robbery to be equal with God, but made Himself of no reputation, taking the form of a bondservant, and coming in the likeness of men. And being found in appearance as a man, He humbled Himself and became obedient to the point of death, even the death of the cross. Therefore God also has highly exalted Him and given Him the name which is above every name, that at the name of Jesus every knee should bow, of those in heaven, and of those on earth, and of those under the earth, and that every tongue should confess that Jesus Christ is Lord, to the glory of God the Father" (2:5–11).

B. In scholarly circles, this passage is known as the Kenotic Hymn.

C. The Greek word *kenosis,* which is found in this passage, means "an emptying."

D. The emphasis of the passage is the transition that Jesus underwent by leaving His exalted state and becoming incarnate.

E. The pattern found in this passage is the pattern of humiliation and exaltation.

F. Jesus began exalted in heaven, but He condescended to join us in our predicament in order to redeem us.

G. By entering into human flesh, He underwent profound humiliation.

H. Throughout His life, the humiliation became worse and worse until it reached its nadir in the cross.

I. After the crucifixion, He was resurrected and exalted to glory once again.

V. The Kenosis

A. In Romans 8, Paul told Christians that unless we are willing to identify with the humiliation of Jesus, we will never share in His exaltation.

B. The Son was willing to empty Himself and make Himself of no reputation.

C. In the nineteenth century, liberal scholars proposed the kenotic theory of the incarnation, saying that the Son's incarnation resulted in the laying aside of His divine attributes, such as omniscience and omnipotence.

D. But the divine nature did not lose its attributes in the incarnation.

    E. The human nature was truly human, and the divine nature remained fully and completely divine.

    F. He emptied Himself of glory, privilege, and exaltation.

VI. Exaltation to Former Glory

    A. After His humiliation, Jesus was again highly exalted.

    B. In His High Priestly Prayer, Jesus asked the Father to restore to Him the glory that He had from the beginning (John 17:5).

    C. This was exactly what the Father did once Jesus completed His work.

    D. In Philippians 2:9, Paul wrote, "Therefore God also has highly exalted Him and given Him the name which is above every name."

    E. Many assume that the name referred to here is *Jesus*.

    F. In fact, the name above every name is the title belonging only to God, namely, *Adonai* ("Lord").

    G. The name *Adonai* is given to Jesus.

BIBLE STUDY

1. Was the plan of redemption included in the eternal decree or counsel of God? What do the following texts indicate?

    a. Ephesians 1:4–11

    b. Ephesians 3:11

    c. 2 Thessalonians 2:13

    d. 2 Timothy 1:9

    e. James 2:5

    f. 1 Peter 1:2

2. Did the plan of salvation have the nature of a covenant? What do the following texts teach us?

    a. John 5:30, 43

    b. John 6:38–40

    c. John 17:4–12

3. How do Romans 5:12–21 and 1 Corinthians 15:22 support the idea that the eternal plan of redemption is a covenant?

4. What do the following texts have in common?

    a. John 6:38–39

    b. John 10:18

    c. John 17:4

    d. Luke 22:29

5. John 1:1–14 is one of the most significant New Testament texts dealing directly with the incarnation. Read these verses and outline the main points that are made in each section.

DISCUSSION GUIDE

1. What was the role of the Father in the covenant of redemption? The Son? The Holy Spirit?

2. Regarding whether the parties to the covenant of grace are God and Christ or God and His people, Charles Hodge said, "The Westminster standards seem to adopt sometimes the one and sometimes the other mode of expression." He argued that in the Confession (7:3), "the implication is that God and his people are the parties."[2] The Larger Catechism, however, says that the covenant of grace "was made with Christ as the second Adam, and in him with all the elect as his seed."[3] Are the two ideas contradictory? Inconsistent? Why or why not?

3. Louis Berkhof argued that it is better to say that the Word became flesh rather than saying that God became man. It is better, he said, because it was the second person of the Trinity who assumed human nature, not the Triune God.[4] Do you agree? Why or why not?

APPLICATION

1. Reflect on the fact that the Father, Son, and Holy Spirit planned your redemption from all eternity. Give praise to God for His amazing grace toward you.

2. The nadir of Christ's humiliation was the cross on which He cried out as He who knew no sin was made sin, and the wrath of God was poured out on Him. Meditate on the following poem, which reminds us that Jesus cried out as one forsaken in order that you and I may never have to.

> *Yea, once, Immanuel's orphaned cry his universe hath shaken—*
> *It went up single, echoless, "My God, I am forsaken!"*
> *It went up from the Holy's lips amid his lost creation,*
> *That, of the lost, no son should use those words of desolation!*[5]

SUGGESTED READING FOR FURTHER STUDY

Athanasius. *On the Incarnation.*

Bavinck, Herman. *Reformed Dogmatics,* vol. 3, pp. 212–16, 323–482.

Berkhof, Louis. *Systematic Theology,* pp. 265–71, 331–55.

Dabney, Robert L. *Systematic Theology,* pp. 431–39.

Hodge, Charles. *Systematic Theology,* vol. 2, pp. 357–62, 378–407.

Kelly, Douglas. *Systematic Theology,* vol. 1, pp. 398–400.

Macleod, Donald. *The Person of Christ,* pp. 155–80.

Owen, John. *The Death of Death in the Death of Christ,* pp. 51–67.

Reymond, Robert. *Jesus, Divine Messiah,* pp. 251–66.

Shedd, William G. T. *Dogmatic Theology,* 3rd edition, pp. 678–80.

Witsius, Herman. *The Economy of the Covenants between God and Man,* vol. 1, pp. 165–92.

NOTES: CHAPTER 1

1. A. E. Biedermann, quoted in Fred G. Zaspel, *The Theology of B. B. Warfield: A Systematic Summary* (Wheaton, IL: Crossway, 2010), 273.

2. Charles Hodge, *Systematic Theology,* vol. 2 (London: Thomas Nelson, 1872), 358.

3. "Q. 31," *The Larger Catechism* (Edinburgh: Thomas Nelson, 1860), 140.

4. Louis Berkhof, *Systematic Theology* (Grand Rapids, MI: Eerdmans, 1996), 333.

5. Elizabeth Barrett Browning, "Cowper's Grave," *Poems,* vol. 3 (London: Chapman & Hall, 1856), 120.

2

INFANCY HYMNS

WE FIND THE NARRATIVES of Jesus' birth in the gospels of
Matthew and Luke, but Luke's account is the more detailed. Luke
alone provides background on John the Baptist's birth; on the
angel Gabriel's announcement to Mary that she was to conceive
and bring forth a Son, who would be the Son of God; on Mary's
visit to Elizabeth, mother of John the Baptist; on the experience
of the shepherds outside Bethlehem; and on Mary and Joseph's
encounters with Simeon and Anna.

Another fascinating feature of Luke's accounts is his inclu-
sion of three songs that were given under the inspiration of the
Holy Spirit. I think these songs are very significant with respect
to the work of Christ, but that significance is often overlooked. In
the Old Testament, when God performed particularly significant

works of deliverance or redemption, His people often celebrated in song. We find the Song of Moses (Exod. 15:1–18), the Song of Miriam (v. 21), and the Song of Deborah (Judg. 5:1–31). In the New Testament, in the book of Revelation, the Apostle John shared his vision of the people of God singing "a new song" (5:9–10).

In Luke, we find three songs that were composed spontaneously to celebrate the incarnation. Each of these songs is known by the first words of the song in Latin. They are the Song of Mary (the *Magnificat*), the Song of Zacharias (the *Benedictus*), and the Song of Simeon (the *Nunc Dimittis*). In this chapter, I want to look briefly at these songs, because their content reveals significant dimensions of the work of Jesus.

THE SONG OF MARY

The Song of Mary, the Magnificat, is perhaps the most famous of the three. Mary, having learned of her pregnancy from Gabriel, and of the pregnancy of her relative Elizabeth with John the Baptist, went to visit Elizabeth. When Mary arrived and greeted Elizabeth, the unborn John leaped in Elizabeth's womb for joy, and Elizabeth welcomed Mary as "the mother of my Lord." Mary then sang:

> My soul magnifies the Lord,
> And my spirit has rejoiced in God my Savior.
> For He has regarded the lowly state of His maidservant;
> For behold, henceforth all generations will call me blessed.

For He who is mighty has done great things for me,

And holy is His name.

And His mercy is on those who fear Him

From generation to generation.

He has shown strength with His arm;

He has scattered the proud in the imagination of their hearts.

He has put down the mighty from their thrones,

And exalted the lowly.

He has filled the hungry with good things,

And the rich He has sent away empty.

He has helped His servant Israel,

In remembrance of His mercy,

As He spoke to our fathers,

To Abraham and to his seed forever. (Luke 1:46b–55)

Mary began by "magnifying" God. Why did she do this? First, she did this because "He has regarded the lowly state of His maidservant" (v. 48a). Mary was overwhelmed that out of all of the women in the history of the world, she, a simple peasant girl, had been selected by God to be the mother of the Messiah. It is as if she was saying, "I can't get over this. He has noticed me. He has regarded me in my low estate." This is the original Cinderella story, that tale of a scullery maid who captured the heart of the prince.

Mary continued: "Behold, henceforth all generations will call me blessed. For He who is mighty has done great things for me, and holy is His name. And His mercy is on those who fear Him from generation to generation" (vv. 48b–50). She knew that it was "the Holy One" who had noticed her and given her such an unspeakable privilege. When the angel told her that she was going to conceive this baby, she was baffled and asked, "How can this be, since I do not know a man?" The angel replied, "With God nothing will be impossible" (1:34, 37). The One who brought the universe and teeming life out of nothing is able to make life in a womb. So Mary celebrated the breathtaking power of God and mercy of God.

"He has shown strength with His arm," Mary sang. "He has scattered the proud in the imagination of their hearts. He has put down the mighty from their thrones, and exalted the lowly. He has filled the hungry with good things, and the rich He has sent away empty" (Luke 1:51–53). Mary understood that if all the weapons of the world were placed in opposition to God, He could sweep them away with one gesture of His mighty right arm. He can scatter the mighty. He can pull down the proud from their seats of power, strip them of their strength, and exalt the lowly. He has fed the hungry but left the rich destitute.

Mary said, "He has helped His servant Israel, in remembrance of His mercy, as He spoke to our fathers, to Abraham and to his seed forever" (vv. 54–55). Here at the end of her song, Mary tied together what she had heard from the angel and from Elizabeth with the nation of Israel. She understood that the baby who had been conceived in her womb was not for an isolated purpose in history, but was the fulfillment of the whole of the Old Testament, the whole expectation of the nation of Israel.

The New Testament speaks of Jesus' birth happening in "the fullness of the time" (Gal. 4:4; Eph. 1:10). This means that the incarnation of Christ was not an afterthought or an impulse of God. Rather, it was part of God's plan, for He had promised His people a redemption tied up together with the covenant that He had made with the patriarch Abraham. That plan was carefully mapped out, so that a definite time was set for Jesus to be born.

When a woman becomes pregnant, her doctor typically sets a "due date." The mother then counts down the months, weeks, and days until the time arrives for the baby to be delivered. Of course, not all babies honor their due dates. Our first child kept us waiting ten days past her due date, and I thought I would lose my mind because I was so eager for the time to be finished so I could see our child. But Jesus came precisely on the due date set in eternity past by the Father.

Just as I was eager for the birth of my daughter, there is a sense in which the whole of history was waiting and groaning for the birth of Jesus, but He could not come until the time had been filled to its capacity. I like to think of this idea of "the fullness of time" as a glass filled to the brim with water. Usually, when we fill a glass with water, we do not fill it all the way to the top; we leave a little space so we can move it around without spilling the water within. But "fullness of time" is like a glass filled to the very brim, so full that it cannot receive one more drop of water without overflowing. In the same way, God so decreed and prepared the world that Jesus came at the precise moment of His pleasure, not one second too soon or too late.

THE SONG OF ZACHARIAS

Similar themes are found in the Benedictus, the Song of Zacharias, who was the father of John the Baptist. Zacharias did not believe the angel who announced that he would have a son who would be the forerunner of the Messiah, so he was struck dumb (Luke 1:19–20). His muteness lasted until the day John was circumcised, when Zacharias's tongue was loosed and he sang:

> Blessed is the Lord God of Israel,
> For He has visited and redeemed His people,
> And has raised up a horn of salvation for us
> In the house of His servant David,
> As He spoke by the mouth of His holy prophets,
> Who have been since the world began,
> That we should be saved from our enemies
> And from the hand of all who hate us,
> To perform the mercy promised to our fathers
> And to remember His holy covenant,
> The oath which He swore to our father Abraham:
> To grant us that we,
> Being delivered from the hand of our enemies,
> Might serve Him without fear,
> In holiness and righteousness before Him all the days of our
>   life.
> And you, child, will be called the prophet of the Highest;
> For you will go before the face of the Lord to prepare His ways,

To give knowledge of salvation to His people
By the remission of their sins,
Through the tender mercy of our God,
With which the Dayspring from on high has visited us;
To give light to those who sit in darkness and the shadow of
　　death,
To guide our feet into the way of peace. (Luke 1:68–79)

Notice the words with which Zacharias began this song: "Blessed is the Lord God of Israel, for He has visited and redeemed His people, and has raised up a horn of salvation for us in the house of His servant David, as He spoke by the mouth of His holy prophets, who have been since the world began" (vv. 68–70). Here Zacharias focused on the visitation of God. The Greek word that is translated as "visited" here is closely related to the Greek word *episkopos,* which usually is translated "bishop" or "overseer." The Episcopal Church is called by that name because bishops govern it. The root of *episkopos* is *skopos,* which means "observer" or "watchman." It is the word from which we get the English word *scope,* which is something we look through to see a thing we are unable to see with the naked eye. A microscope reveals tiny things, a telescope reveals distant things, and so on. The prefix *epi* intensifies the meaning of the root. So, an *episkopos* is someone or something that looks intently, forcibly, and fully at what is being examined.

In the ancient Greek world, the *episkopos* was the general of the army. He would come to the military bases and review the troops. He would inspect them to see whether they were ready for battle. If the troops were not ready, the *episkopos* imposed punishments. If they were ready, he gave praise and rewards.

The New Testament refers to Jesus as our *Episkopos* when it calls Him the "Bishop of your souls" (1 Pet. 2:25 KJV); that means He is our supervisor. He sees all that is taking place in the midst of His people.

The Jews longed for the time when God Himself would visit this planet. They feared that His visit would be a day of darkness if He came and His people were not ready, but they also hoped God would visit His people to redeem them. It is this kind of visit that Zacharias celebrated: "He has visited and redeemed His people." He was thinking not of the bad news of impending judgment but the great news of a redeeming visit by God. Remember, Jesus was called Immanuel, which means "God with us" (Matt. 1:23). So, this hymn celebrates the visitation of God in the incarnation.

Zacharias continued: "That we should be saved from our enemies and from the hand of all who hate us, to perform the mercy promised to our fathers and to remember His holy covenant, the oath which He swore to our father Abraham: to grant us that we, being delivered from the hand of our enemies, might serve Him without fear, in holiness and righteousness before Him all the days of our life" (Luke 1:71–75). Just as Mary did in the Magnificat, Zacharias tied the coming of Christ to the covenant that God made with Abraham. The people waited century after century, but finally, both Mary and Zacharias said the wait was over. God had remembered, for He never forgets His covenants. That is the basis on which we live.

Zacharias then spoke of John the Baptist: "And you, child, will be called the prophet of the Highest; for you will go before the face of the Lord to prepare His ways, to give knowledge of salvation to His people by the remission of their sins" (vv. 76–77).

Here we get a clue as to how God's work of salvation was going to be accomplished; whatever else it involved, it would include a remission of sins, a removal of transgressions from the people of God as far as the east is from the west (Ps. 103:12). It would be done, Zacharias said, "through the tender mercy of our God, with which the Dayspring from on high has visited us" (Luke 1:78). "Dayspring from on high" is a title for Jesus. He is like the star that brightens the dawn "to give light to those who sit in darkness and the shadow of death, to guide our feet into the way of peace" (v. 79).

THE SONG OF SIMEON

There is one other brief hymn in the birth narratives of Luke's gospel—the Nunc Dimittis. The Latin here is the first two words of Simeon's prayer: "Now dismiss." When Mary and Joseph brought the baby Jesus into the temple in Jerusalem for consecration, they met an old man named Simeon. Luke said that he was "just and devout," that the Holy Spirit was on him, and that God had told him he would not die until he saw the Christ (Luke 2:25–26). We do not know how he lived out his days in and about the temple, but I suspect he came every day looking for the Messiah, finding the promise unfulfilled day in, day out, week in, week out, year by year. Finally, one day, the Holy Spirit led him into the temple, where he found Mary and Joseph, then took Jesus in his arms. He then sang: "Lord, now You are letting Your servant depart in peace, according to Your word; for my eyes have seen Your salvation which You have prepared before the face of all peoples, a light to bring revelation to the Gentiles, and the glory of Your people Israel" (vv. 29–32).

The people of Israel had groaned in pain, war, strife, and subjection, looking to God for their salvation. When Simeon held the infant Jesus in his arms, he declared that God's salvation had arrived. Jesus was that salvation—but not just for Israel. Although He was, as Simeon said, "the glory" of Israel, He was also "a light to bring revelation to the Gentiles." Jesus was the salvation for people of all tribes, tongues, and nations.

CHAPTER 2

STUDY GUIDE

INTRODUCTION

Throughout the Old Testament, God's major redemptive acts were celebrated in song. The Song of Moses in Exodus 15 celebrated the redemption of Israel from Egypt. The Song of Deborah in Judges 5 celebrated the defeat of the Canaanites. These and other songs are found throughout Israel's history—many in the book of Psalms. All of these earlier redemptive acts, however, paled in comparison to the incarnation of the Son. In this chapter, Dr. R. C. Sproul looks at three songs that celebrated the coming of the Messiah.

LEARNING OBJECTIVES

1. To be able to explain the significance of biblical songs that celebrate God's great acts of redemption.
2. To be able to summarize the main points of the three messianic hymns in the opening chapters of Luke.

QUOTATIONS

And Mary said: "My soul magnifies the Lord, and my spirit has rejoiced in God my Savior. For He has regarded the lowly state of His maidservant; for behold, henceforth all generations will call me blessed. For He who is mighty has done great things for me, and holy is His name. And His mercy is on those who fear Him from generation to generation. He has shown strength with His arm; He has scattered the proud in the imagination of their hearts. He has put down the mighty from their thrones, and exalted the lowly. He has filled the hungry with good things, and the rich He has sent away empty. He has helped His servant Israel, in remembrance of His mercy, as He spoke to our fathers, to Abraham and to his seed forever."

—Luke 1:46–55

What God has done in Christ demands to be praised. It is not enough simply to say what God has done to save us—what he has done also needs to be celebrated in song.

—Philip Graham Ryken, *Luke*

OUTLINE

I. Introduction

    A. In the gospel of Luke, we have the account of three songs celebrating the incarnation.

    B. In our tradition, these songs are known by the first words of each song in Latin.

II. The Magnificat

    A. The song Mary sang after contemplating the announcement by Gabriel is known as the Magnificat.

    B. Mary was overwhelmed that she had been selected to be the mother of the Messiah.

    C. The Holy One of Israel gave her this unspeakable privilege.

    D. Mary celebrated the breathtaking power of God.

    E. Mary declared that God had pulled down the mighty and proud from their seats of power.

F. She understood that this baby was tied to the expectations of Israel.

G. He was born in the fullness *(pleroma)* of time.

H. He was born in fulfillment of the ancient covenantal promises made to Abraham.

III. The Benedictus

A. Similar themes are found in the Song of Zacharias, a song known as the Benedictus.

B. Zacharias focused on the visitation of God.

C. The word *visitation* is based on a verb from which we get the noun translated "bishop."

D. The word *episkopos* is translated "bishop."

E. The parts that form the word *episkopos* literally mean something that looks intently at what is being examined.

F. In the ancient Greek world, the *episkopos* was the general of the army who would come to the military bases and review the troops.

G. The New Testament refers to Jesus as the bishop of our souls.

H. The Jews longed for the day when the Lord Himself would visit.

I. They feared the visitation could be a day of darkness, but they also held out hope that the visitation would be a day of redemption.

J. Zacharias celebrated the birth of Christ as a redeeming visit by God.

K. The Benedictus also ties the coming of Christ to the covenant promises made to Abraham.

L. In his words regarding John, Zacharias explained that the work of salvation would involve the remission of sins.

IV. The Nunc Dimittis

A. The Nunc Dimittis is the brief song Simeon sang when Joseph and Mary brought Jesus to the temple.

B. God had promised Simeon that he would not die until he saw the Messiah—the "consolation of Israel" (Luke 2:25 ESV).

C. When Jesus was brought to the temple, Simeon recognized that the child was the promised Messiah and proceeded to praise God.

BIBLE STUDY

1. Read the Song of Moses in Exodus 15, the Song of Deborah in Judges 5, and the Song of David in 2 Samuel 22. What do these songs teach us about God?

2. Read Hannah's song of praise in 1 Samuel 2:1–10 and Mary's Magnificat in Luke 1:46–55. What parallels do you detect? What differences are evident?

3. What two images of God are prevalent in the Magnificat?

4. Read the Benedictus in Luke 1:68–79. How does Zacharias tie the redemptive roles of John and Jesus together in this song?

5. Read the Nunc Dimittis in Luke 2:29–32. The Magnificat and the Benedictus explicitly mention Christ as the One who fulfills the Abrahamic covenant. In what way does Simeon's brief song implicitly point to Christ as the One who fulfills the Abrahamic covenant (cf. Gen. 12:1–3)?

DISCUSSION GUIDE

1. Many Christians have read and reread the New Testament without ever having read the Old Testament. Having studied the contents of the three songs in Luke 1–2, do you believe we can fully understand the person and work of Christ apart from an understanding of the Old Testament promises?

2. Many Protestants are fearful that any kind of respect for Mary borders on Roman Catholicism. How does the Magnificat

inform a proper understanding of Mary? What should our attitude toward Mary be?

3. When Gabriel foretold the birth of Jesus to Mary, he told her that her Son would be called "Son of the Highest" (Luke 1:32). In the Benedictus, Zacharias said of John that he would be called "prophet of the Highest" (1:76). What is the significance of the difference between these titles?

APPLICATION

1. Martin Luther said that Mary's song was about "the great works and deeds of God, for the strengthening of our faith, for the comforting of all those of low degree, and for the terrifying of all the mighty ones of earth. We are to let the hymn serve this threefold purpose; for she sang it not for herself alone but for us all, to sing it after her."[1] Consider the words of Mary's song. Let these words strengthen your faith; let them comfort you with the truth of God's faithfulness; let them humble your pride. Consider how He who is mighty has done great things not only for Mary, but for you as well, through the death and resurrection of Mary's child, God's Son, Jesus Christ, our Lord.

2. When reading the Benedictus, consider the tender mercy of God toward you, and thank Him for the forgiveness of your sins provided through this One who was born of the virgin Mary.

3. Regarding Simeon (and Anna), J. C. Ryle wrote, "If they, with so few helps and so many discouragements, lived such a life of faith, how much more ought we with a finished Bible and a full Gospel. Let us strive, like them, to walk by faith and look forward."[2]

SUGGESTED READING FOR FURTHER STUDY

Geldenhuys, Norval. *The Gospel of Luke,* pp. 84–88, 92–98, 119.
Ryken, Philip Graham. *Luke,* vol. 1, pp. 41–64, 88–100.

NOTES: CHAPTER 2

1. Jaroslav Pelikan and Helmut T. Lehmann, eds., *Luther's Works,* vol. 21 (St. Louis: Concordia, 1986), 306.
2. J. C. Ryle, *Expository Thoughts on the Gospels,* vol. 1, *St. Luke* (New York: Robert Carter, 1879), 75.

3

JESUS IN THE TEMPLE

THE NEW TESTAMENT TEACHES us almost nothing about the so-called lost years of Jesus, that period between His birth and the beginning of His public ministry around the age of thirty. That silence leaves us to wonder what His life was like as He was growing up in Nazareth, presumably working in the carpenter shop of His earthly father, Joseph. We are given only two accounts of events that happened between His dedication at the temple (Luke 2:22–38) and His baptism (Luke 3:21–22). The first is His family's flight into Egypt soon after His birth, where they remained until the death of Herod the Great (Matt. 2:13–15, 19–23). The second is His visit to Jerusalem at the age of twelve, when He astonished the scholars in the temple with His understanding (Luke 2:41–50). In this chapter, I want to focus on the second incident.

The lost years of Jesus' life are the subject of fanciful apocryphal gospels that were penned in the second and third centuries by the Gnostic heretics. In an attempt to show that they had equal authority to the Apostles, they attached the names of some of the Apostles to their gospels, creating documents such as the gospel of Peter and the gospel of Thomas. The early church repudiated these books because they were not of true Apostolic origin and therefore did not have canonical authority. However, there has been a flurry of interest in them in the years since the appearance of Dan Brown's best-selling novel *The Da Vinci Code,* which includes much speculation drawn from these apocryphal works.

In these books, we frequently find fanciful stories of Jesus as a boy making trivial use of His supernatural powers. For instance, a book called the *First Gospel of the Infancy of Jesus Christ* tells of Jesus forming birds of clay and then bringing them to life. This kind of thing is so plainly apocryphal that it is easily dismissed as a false record of the life of Jesus.

Basically, the canonical gospels tell us that, during His childhood and adolescence, Jesus "grew and became strong in spirit, filled with wisdom; and the grace of God was upon Him" (Luke 2:40; see also v. 52). However, we are given one brief glimpse of that wisdom in Luke's record of Jesus' visit to the temple. Luke wrote:

> His parents went to Jerusalem every year at the Feast
> of the Passover. And when He was twelve years old,

they went up to Jerusalem according to the custom of the feast. When they had finished the days, as they returned, the Boy Jesus lingered behind in Jerusalem. And Joseph and His mother did not know it; but supposing Him to have been in the company, they went a day's journey, and sought Him among their relatives and acquaintances. So when they did not find Him, they returned to Jerusalem, seeking Him. Now so it was that after three days they found Him in the temple, sitting in the midst of the teachers, both listening to them and asking them questions. And all who heard Him were astonished at His understanding and answers. So when they saw Him, they were amazed; and His mother said to Him, "Son, why have You done this to us? Look, Your father and I have sought You anxiously."

And He said to them, "Why did you seek Me? Did you not know that I must be about My Father's business?" But they did not understand the statement which He spoke to them. (2:41–50)

THE MIND OF CHRIST

This passage shows us that the mind of Jesus was radically different from that of everyone else. Why was this so? The biblical teaching on the fall of the human race reveals that the effects of sin permeate the whole person. The fall not only weakened the body severely—so that it is exposed to physical maladies, to diseases, and to death—it also had a significant impact on the human mind. Sin clouds the mind and impairs our ability to think clearly. We call these results of the fall the noetic effects of sin. This concept comes from the Greek word *nous*, which means "mind." The word *noetic* means "of or pertaining to the *nous*" or "of or pertaining to the human mind."

It is not difficult to see examples of how the act of thinking has been weakened by sin. I used to teach a course in logic, and after teaching my students the various kinds of logical fallacies, I would give them the assignment of bringing examples of each fallacy from the local newspaper. It was never difficult for them to find examples of the fallacies we studied. In fact, the textbook we used actually drew examples not from popular journalism but from the greatest minds in the history of the world. We saw logical errors in statements from Plato, René Descartes, Immanuel Kant, David Hume, and John Stuart Mill because all people, even those who are exceedingly bright, are given to making logical errors.

Of course, humanity retained the capacity for reason even after the fall. We can still, even in our sinfulness, add two and two and come to the conclusion that they equal four. We can still work syllogisms and other philosophical problems. Yet each one of us is given to making mistakes in our thinking, mistakes that can be very costly.

I have often wondered why it so often happens that when people are exposed to certain information, they come to such radically different conclusions. Is the Bible so lacking in clarity that people can form vastly different beliefs and hold them with such tenacity as to create divisions and disruptions within the life of the church, the lives of families, and all types of human relationships? We all have the same material, although, of course, some people study more diligently than others, so they are more likely to have a better understanding of the material. But all of us fail to love the Lord our God with all of our minds, and so all of us fall into periods of slothfulness, times when we fail to diligently apply ourselves intellectually to the understanding of Scripture.

Not only that, in our sinful condition, we all come to the text of Scripture with certain biases, and the biased person can often miss the forest for the trees because his or her mind is held in captivity by that bias. If someone is raised in a particular tradition, belongs to a particular church, and is taught the doctrine of that particular church, that person may receive doctrinal teaching that is incorrect, but because it comes from trusted individuals— parents, pastors, beloved Sunday school teachers, and so on—the person is predisposed to internalize those beliefs and cling to them tenaciously. Those "love lines," those prior commitments to certain denominations or certain people, are very hard to cut. They can make it very difficult for us to be open to a better understanding of what Scripture teaches.

Can you imagine a human being functioning mentally with none of the noetic effects of sin? Before Jesus came, the world had never seen a sinless human being. Because Jesus did not participate in original sin, the noetic effects we have been talking about did not weaken His mind. His thinking was crystal clear. His acumen was without parallel. Even as a twelve-year-old child, He could think more profoundly, consistently, and acutely than the most learned theologians of His day. Of course, we know He did not go to the temple to show off. He went there to learn, because that is what He had been doing for the first twelve years of His life.

People sometimes say: "Well, of course Jesus was able to converse with the scholars. He was God, and God is omniscient." Yes, He was God incarnate, and yes, God is omniscient. However, in His human nature, Jesus was not endowed with the divine attribute of omniscience. The divine nature could communicate information to the human nature, which is why, from time to time, we see Jesus astonishing people with the supernatural knowledge that was at His disposal. But the divine nature did not communicate the divine attribute of omniscience to the human nature, as some have tried to argue throughout church history. That would have been a violation of Jesus' true humanity.

JESUS' SENSE OF MISSION

Luke tells us that Jesus' parents went to Jerusalem each year for the Passover Feast. People came from great distances for the Passover, and Jesus' family came from Nazareth, about seventy miles away. They may have taken Jesus when He was younger, but it was customary, a year or two before a boy turned thirteen, for his family to bring him to the temple so that he might become accustomed to the procedures that would be followed at his bar mitzvah.

After the feast, Mary and Joseph left Jerusalem without knowing exactly where Jesus was. When families went to Jerusalem for the feast, they typically traveled in large groups of extended family members and acquaintances, and Jesus' parents seem to have assumed He was somewhere in the group with which they were traveling (v. 44). Finally, when Jesus' absence began to seem too long, they looked for Him in the group but did not find Him. Eventually, they realized He had not come along with the group, so they went back to Jerusalem to look for Him. We can only imagine the anxiety that overcame them as they sought their unusual Son.

It took three days of searching, but they finally found Jesus in the temple in the midst of the teachers. Luke wrote that when they found Him, "His mother said to Him, 'Son, why have You done this to us? Look, Your father and I have sought You anxiously'" (v. 48). Here is an incident that could be used to argue against the sinlessness of Jesus. Apparently, His behavior had upset Mary. She saw His lingering in the temple as a thoughtless offense to her, to her husband, and to the whole family.

When Jesus heard this accusing question, He replied: "Why did you seek Me? Did you not know that I must be about My Father's business?" (v. 49). He was saying, in effect, "You should have known where I was. You should not have had to seek Me." However, "they did not understand the statement which He spoke to them" (v. 50). So, there was a problem of knowledge. Mary and Joseph did not know why He was doing what He was doing. There is a sense that Jesus was mildly and politely rebuking His mother for not knowing what she should have known, particularly in light of all of the revelation that had been given to her, especially at the time of her annunciation. She had been meditating and pondering these things for years (Luke 2:19), wondering about the destiny of her Son, the message that had been given to her by the angel Gabriel, the meaning of the virgin birth, and the words of Simeon and the prophetess Anna.

When Jesus spoke of "My Father's business," He was speaking, of course, of His heavenly Father. These words also give us insight into His work. Even at age twelve, in His growing awareness of His task on earth, He knew He had a job to perform for His Father, and that job had something to do with the temple and the things that were being discussed there.

There is a subordination of sorts between the Son and the Father in the Trinity. Theologians speak about the economic distinctions in the Trinity, the distinctions that have to do with the work of God. The Father sends the Son. The Son comes and accomplishes the work of redemption. The Spirit applies the work of redemption to people. The Son, even at this early stage in His earthly life, was aware of this subordinate responsibility. Furthermore, He had a driving compulsion to do what the Father had sent Him to do. Later on, He would say, "My food is to do the will of Him who sent Me, and to finish His work" (John 4:34). He had a mission, and He was committed to carrying it out.

CHAPTER 3

STUDY GUIDE

INTRODUCTION

The New Testament tells us very little about the years between Jesus' birth and the beginning of His ministry. The gospel of Luke contains the one significant account that exists—the story of Jesus' visit to the temple at the age of twelve. In this chapter, Dr. R. C. Sproul explains what we can learn about the person and work of Christ from this brief narrative.

LEARNING OBJECTIVES

1. To be able to explain the effects of sin on the human mind.
2. To be able to explain how the lack of sin made Jesus unique in terms of His thinking.

QUOTATIONS

> And He said to them, "Why did you seek Me? Did you not know that I must be about My Father's business?"
>
> —Luke 2:49

> It is remarkable that the first words of Jesus quoted in the Gospel narrative are these words in which He so clearly refers to His divine Sonship, and in which He points to His life's vocation to be about His Father's business—to serve and glorify Him in all things and at all times. The words indicate a divine inevitability: Jesus *must* be busy with the interests of His Father. With Him it is, however, not a case of external compulsion—His whole nature yearns to serve and obey His Father voluntarily.
>
> —Norval Geldenhuys, *The Gospel of Luke*

OUTLINE

I. Introduction

    A. The record of Jesus' visit to the temple at the age of twelve usually receives very little attention.

    B. This text is the only passage in the New Testament that tells us anything about this period of Jesus' life.

    C. The apocryphal gospels created in the second and third centuries by the Gnostic heretics often speculated about what happened during Jesus' childhood.

    D. Many of them are filled with fanciful stories that involve Jesus using His power in trivial ways.

II. The Temple Visit

    A. The narrative of Jesus' childhood visit to the temple is recorded in Luke 2:41–52.

    B. This episode emphasizes the response of the theologians of Jesus' day to His incredible knowledge of Scripture and theology.

III. The Noetic Effects of Sin

    A. The knowledge of Jesus was radically different from everyone else's.

B. In the fall, the effects of sin permeated the whole human person.

C. The fall had a significant impact upon the minds of human beings.

D. In theology, the effect of the fall on the mind is called the noetic effect of sin.

E. The word *noetic* comes from the Greek word *nous,* which means "mind."

F. Sin clouds the mind and impairs our ability to think clearly.

G. We still have the capacity for reason, yet at the same time, all of us make mistakes in our thinking.

H. Even though Christians have the same Bible, we disagree, sometimes seriously, about the meaning of certain parts of the Bible.

I. All of us fail to apply ourselves as seriously as we could to the study of Scripture.

J. We also come to the text of Scripture with biases that are difficult to overcome.

K. The very act of thinking has been weakened by sin.

L. Before Jesus, no one's mind had functioned apart from these noetic effects of sin.

M. Jesus was not weakened by any of these effects because Jesus was not impacted by original sin.

N. As a twelve-year-old, He could think more profoundly than the most learned theologians of His day.

IV. Fully Human and Fully Divine

A. Some say that Jesus was so profound in His thinking because He was God and God is omniscient.

B. He was God incarnate, and God is omniscient, but in His human nature, Jesus was not given a divine brain.

C. He was not endowed in His human nature with the divine attribute of omniscience.

D. The divine nature did not communicate the divine attribute of omniscience to the human nature.

V. In My Father's House

A. According to the text of Luke's gospel, Jesus was brought to the temple at the age of twelve.

B. After Mary and Joseph left and had been traveling for an entire day, they noticed Jesus was not with them.

C. They returned to Jerusalem, and after three days of searching, they found Him in the temple in the midst of the teachers there.

D. The teachers were amazed at His understanding.

E. When Mary asked Him why He did this, Jesus said, "Why did you seek Me? Did you not know that I must be about My Father's business?" (Luke 2:49).

F. Jesus was politely rebuking His mother for not knowing what she should have known in light of all the revelation she had received.

G. Even at the age of twelve, Jesus knew that He had a task to perform.

H. He was subordinate to the Father, not in respect of His being, but in respect of the work He was called to do.

BIBLE STUDY

1. Read the entire account of Jesus' visit to the temple in Luke 2:41–52. What is the one overarching point that is made in this passage of Scripture?

2. There is some ambiguity in the translation of the words Jesus spoke, because the Greek reads literally: "Did you not know that I must be in the ... of My Father?" Three interpretations have been suggested:

    a. Jesus said He must be among those of His Father's house, that is, among the Jewish teachers of the law.

    b. Jesus said He must be about His Father's business.

    c. Jesus said He must be in His Father's house; that is, He must be involved with instruction in divine things.

Based on the context, what are the strengths and weaknesses of each proposed interpretation? Which do you find most persuasive? Why?

3. The words Jesus spoke in verse 49 are the first words of Jesus recorded in Scripture. All of the other recorded words of Christ were spoken after the beginning of His ministry. Assuming the correctness of the translation "I must be in My Father's house," how are these words significant to our understanding of the person and work of Christ?

DISCUSSION GUIDE

1. It is not unreasonable to assume that some of the teachers mentioned in this text, teachers who were amazed at Jesus' understanding, were still alive when He began His public ministry eighteen years later. According to the Gospels, however, the reaction to Jesus by the Jewish teachers at that time was largely hostile. What accounts for the different response?

2. How does a proper doctrine of the relationship between Jesus' divine and human natures help us understand the words of Luke 2:52?

3. What are some of the ways that the noetic effects of sin contribute to doctrinal disagreements among Bible-believing Christians?

APPLICATION

1. Although He was the Son of God, Jesus submitted to His earthly parents (Luke 2:51). Strive to demonstrate the same kind of humble submission to those in authority over you.

2. Because Jesus accomplished the work given to Him by His Father, we can now also call God our Father. Give praise to God for this amazing privilege.

SUGGESTED READING FOR FURTHER STUDY

Geldenhuys, Norval. *The Gospel of Luke,* pp. 125–32.
Ryken, Philip Graham. *Luke,* vol. 1, pp. 101–13.

4

BAPTISM

WHEN JOHN THE BAPTIST appeared and began to call the people of Israel to undergo baptism, he was doing something radical. In fact, his ministry was radical in multiple ways.

In the first place, the voice of prophecy in Israel had been silent for four hundred years. We have a tendency to look back into the past and telescope history, and that tendency causes us to assume that, in Old Testament Israel, miracles happened every day and prophets appeared every other Friday. The prophets had a very high and important role in the life of the people of God, but the office of prophet had seemingly ceased with Malachi; after him about four centuries went by with no word from God, no special revelation. Four hundred years is a long time. As I write this, it has not yet been four hundred years since the Pilgrims came to the shores of America. A lot of history transpires over the course of four centuries.

But suddenly, after four hundred years of divine silence, John appeared, coming from the desert, the traditional meeting place of God and His prophets. He wore the kind of clothing—camel's hair and a leather belt (Matt. 3:4)—that the Jews associated with the asceticism of certain prophets in the Old Testament. Above all, he spoke as one having the authority of God. He quickly caused great excitement among people in Israel because he represented the restoration of the voice of prophecy.

However, the most radical thing about John was not the fact that he was a prophet, the way he dressed, or the way he spoke. It was what he did. Specifically, he called the people of Israel to the Jordan River to be baptized.

It is important to note that the baptism John administered was not identical to the baptism that Jesus introduced in the new-covenant church. Yes, there are certain links between them, but John's baptism was associated with Old Testament ideas. In the Old Testament, the Jews had a ritual called proselyte baptism, which was applied to Gentiles who were converting to Judaism. In Jewish categories, the Gentiles were regarded as strangers to the old covenant. They were outside the covenant community of Israel, so they were considered to be unclean, impure, and defiled. Thus, if Gentiles wanted to convert to Judaism, they had to go through certain procedures, including proselyte baptism. This was a cleansing ritual designed to remove the Gentile's ceremonial impurity.

With that background, we can see how radical it was for John to call not Gentiles but Israelites to undergo baptism. He was doing the unthinkable. After all, the Jews saw themselves as ceremonially clean, having no need for cleansing. Therefore, John's call greatly offended the Pharisees and the other religious leaders of the Jews who went out from Jerusalem to see what John was doing. John warned them: "Brood of vipers! Who warned you to flee from the wrath to come? Therefore bear fruits worthy of repentance, and do not think to say to yourselves, 'We have Abraham as our father.' For I say to you that God is able to raise up children to Abraham from these stones" (Matt. 3:7b–9).

Why did John have this ministry? In the Old Testament, the prophets, particularly Isaiah, talked about the coming of the Messiah, but they also foretold that before the Messiah would arrive, there would be a forerunner, one who would prepare the way for the Messiah. John was that one anointed by God to cry as a voice in the wilderness: "Prepare the way of the LORD; make His paths straight" (Matt. 3:3b).

John's message was simple. He told the people, "Repent, for the kingdom of heaven is at hand!" (Matt. 3:2). The prophets had spoken of the kingdom of God, and the Jews longed to see it, but they thought of it as something in the nebulous, far-off future. No specific time frame had been given for the coming of the kingdom and the Messiah. Then John came and declared, "The kingdom of God is about to break through."

AN IMPENDING ARRIVAL

John used vivid metaphors and images to convey the urgency of the moment. He said, "Even now the ax is laid to the root of the trees. Therefore every tree which does not bear good fruit is cut down and thrown into the fire" (Matt. 3:10). Here John used the image of a woodsman who intends to chop down a tree. But in John's image, the woodsman was not sharpening his ax and thinking about cutting down the tree. Neither had he given the tree one or two strokes. Rather, the ax had cut nearly all the way through the tree, to the very center, and the tree was ready to topple.

Likewise, John said, "He who is coming after me is mightier than I.... His winnowing fan is in His hand, and He will thoroughly clean out His threshing floor, and gather His wheat into the barn; but He will burn up the chaff with unquenchable fire" (Matt. 3:11–12). Here the picture was of a farmer who had harvested his wheat and was prepared to separate the wheat from the chaff. The wheat was in a big pile and had been beaten to separate the seed from the chaff, the husk. After that, the farmer would take his winnowing fork and toss the mix of seed and chaff into the air, and the breeze would blow away the chaff while the heavier seed fell back into the pile. Again, John's metaphor conveyed urgency; he said the farmer had his winnowing fork in hand and was ready to go to work on the pile.

The crisis moment of separation had arrived.

John was warning the people of God. He was telling them that their King, their Messiah, was at the threshold, but they were not ready. They were unclean. So, through the mouth of the prophet John the Baptist, God imposed a new regulation on the people of Israel—they, like the Gentiles, had to be made clean in preparation for the coming of the King.

John's teaching sparked speculation that he himself was the Messiah, but John denied that. John's gospel tells us:

> Now this is the testimony of John, when the Jews sent priests and Levites from Jerusalem to ask him, "Who are you?" He confessed, and did not deny, but confessed, "I am not the Christ." And they asked him, "What then? Are you Elijah?" He said, "I am not." "Are you the Prophet?" And he answered, "No." Then they said to him, "Who are you, that we may give an answer to those who sent us? What do you say about yourself?" He said: "I am 'The voice of one crying in the wilderness: Make straight the way of the LORD,' as the prophet Isaiah said." Now those who were sent were from the Pharisees. And they asked him, saying, "Why then do you baptize if you are not the Christ, nor Elijah, nor the Prophet?" John answered them, saying, "I baptize with water, but there stands One among you whom you do not know. It is He who, coming after me, is preferred before me, whose sandal strap I am not worthy to loose." These things were done in Bethabara beyond the Jordan, where John was baptizing. The next

day John saw Jesus coming toward him, and said,
"Behold! The Lamb of God who takes away the sin
of the world!" (1:19–29)

John denied that he was the Messiah, Elijah, or the Prophet
(a great prophet foretold by Moses in Deut.18:15). Instead, he
explained that he was the forerunner of the Messiah, who would
be infinitely greater than John himself.

Then, the day after John explained all this, he saw Jesus
coming toward him and pointed Him out as the Lamb of God,
the One who would take away sin through sacrificing Himself.
The biggest problem the Jews had with their understanding of
the Messiah was the element of sacrifice. They saw the Messiah
as a conquering king. But John compared Jesus to a lamb in
His redemptive work. As every Jew knew, lambs were used for
sacrifice.

John continued:

> This is He of whom I said, "After me comes a Man
> who is preferred before me, for He was before me." I
> did not know Him; but that He should be revealed
> to Israel, therefore I came baptizing with water.... I
> saw the Spirit descending from heaven like a dove,
> and He remained upon Him. I did not know Him,
> but He who sent me to baptize with water said to
> me, "Upon whom you see the Spirit descending, and
> remaining on Him, this is He who baptizes with the

Holy Spirit." And I have seen and testified that this
is the Son of God. (John 1:30–34)

Here John recounted his baptism of Jesus. He said that baptism was accompanied by a sign—the Holy Spirit in the form of a
dove descended from heaven and rested on Him—and that God
had told John to watch for that very sign, for it would identify the
Messiah. Thus, in a sense, John's ministry of baptism was about
identifying the Messiah so that he might proclaim Him as the
Lamb of God.

However, the fact that the Spirit rested on Jesus at His baptism
is very significant in and of itself. It means that the work of Christ
was not done by the divine nature thinly clothed in the human
nature. It was the human Jesus who was anointed by the Holy
Spirit to fulfill the mission of the Messiah.

Jesus' baptism by John marked the beginning of His public
ministry. It was, as it were, His ordination. God had sent Him
to be the fulfillment of the prophecies of the Messiah, but He
did not enter into that mission until He was baptized. At His
baptism, He was anointed to fulfill the prophecy of Isaiah 61,
which says, "The Spirit of the Lord GOD is upon Me, because
the LORD has anointed Me to preach good tidings to the poor;
He has sent Me to heal the brokenhearted, to proclaim liberty
to the captives, and the opening of the prison to those who are
bound; to proclaim the acceptable year of the LORD" (vv. 1–2a).
When Jesus began His ministry by preaching in the synagogue of
Nazareth, He quoted this text (Luke 4:16–19) and then told the

congregation, "Today this Scripture is fulfilled in your hearing" (v. 21). The people should have known that He was saying, "I am the Messiah," but they rejected Him.

FULFILLING ALL RIGHTEOUSNESS

Matthew's account of the baptism of Jesus provides a small detail that I believe is of the utmost importance for understanding the significance of this event in Jesus' mission. We read: "Then Jesus came from Galilee to John at the Jordan to be baptized by him. And John tried to prevent Him, saying, 'I need to be baptized by You, and are You coming to me?'" (3:13–14). John had been sent as the herald of the Messiah, to announce His arrival. He never expected that he would baptize Jesus. He felt that Jesus should baptize him. As we noted above, he said that the One "coming after me, is preferred before me, whose sandal strap I am not worthy to loose" (John 1:27). John knew who Jesus was and understood fully that He had no need to undergo a cleansing ritual.

Jesus, however, did not have time to instruct John in theology at that point. Matthew tells us that "Jesus answered and said to him, 'Permit it to be so now, for thus it is fitting for us to fulfill all righteousness.' Then he allowed Him" (v. 15). Jesus asked John to trust Him and to baptize Him, for by doing so they would "fulfill all righteousness."

In all of the New Testament, I do not think there is any more important text defining the work of Jesus. It tells us that Jesus was sent to fulfill all righteousness. For the Jews, that meant obeying every jot and tittle of the law. In undergoing baptism, Jesus was not acting for Himself but for His people. Since His people were required to keep the Ten Commandments, He had to keep the Ten Commandments. Likewise, since His people were now required, according to the command of the prophet John the Baptist, to submit to this baptismal ritual, He had to submit to it.

Jesus had to adhere to the whole law of God because the redemption He brought was not accomplished solely by His death on the cross. God did not send Jesus to earth on Good Friday so He could go straight to the cross. Jesus not only had to die for our sins, but also had to live for our righteousness. If Jesus had only died for our sins, His sacrifice would have removed all of our guilt, but that would have left us merely sinless in the sight of God, not righteous. We would not have done anything to obey the law of God, which is righteousness.

In theology, we distinguish between the passive obedience of Jesus and His active obedience. The passive obedience of Christ was His willingness to submit to the pain that the Father inflicted on Him as He hung on the cross. He passively received the curse of God there. His active obedience was His whole life of obeying the law of God, whereby He qualified to be the Savior. It was by His perfect obedience that He became the Lamb without blemish.

The covenant with Moses declared that everyone who fulfilled the law received the blessing and that those who disobeyed the law received the curse. What did Jesus do? He obeyed the law perfectly, so He earned the blessing and not the curse. At the cross, our sin was transferred to His account and was laid upon Him. That meant He received the curse, not the blessing. But in our redemption, His righteousness is imputed to us, so we receive the blessing and not the curse we deserve. Jesus would not have had that righteousness if He had not lived a life of perfect obedience.

The bottom line is that Jesus' life of perfect obedience was just as necessary for our salvation as His perfect atonement on the cross. The reason is that there is a double imputation: our sin to Him and His righteousness to us. That is what Scripture is getting at when it says, "THE LORD OUR RIGHTEOUSNESS" (Jer. 33:16).

John the Baptist did not understand that truth when Jesus came to him to be baptized, but he understands it now. To fulfill all the law, Jesus had to submit to baptism.

CHAPTER 4

STUDY GUIDE

INTRODUCTION

After four hundred years of silence, the voice of prophecy resumed in Israel with the arrival of John the Baptist. He came, calling all Israel to repent and be baptized. Jesus' baptism by John marks the official beginning of His public ministry. In this chapter, Dr. R. C. Sproul looks closely at the baptism of Jesus, explaining how significant it was in His life and how relevant it is for our salvation.

LEARNING OBJECTIVES

1. To be able to explain the significance of the baptism of Jesus in His public ministry.
2. To be able to explain why it was necessary for Jesus to fulfill all righteousness.

QUOTATIONS

> So here is Jesus, at the beginning of his ministry as at its close, numbered among the transgressors, not ashamed to call them his brothers and placing himself under the law to redeem those who are under the law. A trinity of condescension, love and grace combine in this moment of theophany as the God-man, clothes dripping from his standing in Jordan's streams, receives a shower of blessing from on high.
>
> —Iain Campbell, *Opening Up Matthew's Gospel*

The most obvious way in which Jesus' baptism prepares for his mission is by indicating his solidarity with John's call to repentance in view of the arrival of God's kingship. By first identifying with John's proclamation Jesus lays the foundation for his own mission to take on where John has left off. Further, as Jesus is baptized along with others at the Jordan, he is identified with all those who by accepting John's baptism have declared their desire for a new beginning with God. He thus prepares for his own role in "bearing their weaknesses" (8:17) and eventually "giving his life as a ransom for many" (20:28) through shedding his blood for their forgiveness (26:28). If he is to be their representative, he must first be identified with them.

—R. T. France, *The Gospel of Matthew*

OUTLINE

I. Introduction

A. The beginning of Jesus' public ministry occurred at His baptism by John the Baptist.

B. It is important to realize the radical nature of this event.

II. John the Baptist

A. John arrived on the scene after the voice of prophecy had been silent for some four hundred years.

B. John came out of the desert, the traditional meeting place between God and the prophets, and spoke as one having authority from God.

C. The most radical thing John did was to call the people of Israel to be baptized.

D. At this time, proselyte baptism was required of Gentiles who wanted to join the covenant community of Israel.

E. They were baptized because they were considered unclean.

F. John came along and began calling Jews to submit to a cleansing ritual.

G. His message greatly offended the Pharisees and other religious leaders.

H. The prophets had said there would be a forerunner who would prepare the way for the Messiah.

I. John was the forerunner.

J. He called the people to repent because the kingdom of God was at hand.

K. The King was about to appear, the Messiah was at the door, and Israel was not ready because she was unclean.

III. The Baptism of Jesus

A. When John saw Jesus approaching, he said, "Behold! The Lamb of God who takes away the sin of the world!" (John 1:29).

B. This aspect of Jesus' ministry caused the Jews the most difficulty; they could not grasp how the Messiah could be a sacrificial lamb.

C. Jesus' baptism marked the beginning of His ministry; it was His ordination, as it were.

D. At His baptism, He was anointed in order to fulfill Isaiah 61.

E. The human Jesus was anointed by the Holy Spirit to fulfill the mission of the Messiah.

F. John tried to prevent Jesus' baptism at first because baptism was for sinners.

G. Jesus did not explain everything to John but merely said, "Permit it to be so now, for thus it is fitting for us to fulfill all righteousness" (Matt. 3:15).

IV. To Fulfill All Righteousness

A. This statement that Jesus made in response to John is crucial for understanding the work of Christ.

B. It meant that Jesus was to obey every jot and tittle of the law.

C. He submitted to baptism on His people's behalf because He not only had to die for their sins, but also had to live for their righteousness.

D. If Jesus only died for your sins, that would leave you sinless, but not righteous.

E. The passive obedience of Christ refers to His willing submission to the wrath of God on the cross.

F. The active obedience of Christ refers to His whole life of obeying the law.

G. Jesus obeyed the law perfectly, and thereby received the blessing rather than the curse.

H. Our sin was imputed to Him on the cross.

I. His righteousness was imputed to us, but He would not have had this righteousness if He hadn't lived a life of perfect obedience.

J. This is double imputation.

BIBLE STUDY

1. According to John 1:31, why did John come baptizing with water? How would his work of baptizing with water accomplish this goal?

2. Read Matthew 3:2, and compare this message of John with the following Old Testament texts:

  a. Isaiah 31:6; 45:22; 55:7
  b. Jeremiah 3:7, 10, 14, 22; 4:1; 8:5; 18:11; 24:7; 25:5; 26:3; 35:15; 36:7; 44:5
  c. Ezekiel 13:22; 14:6; 18:23, 30; 33:9
  d. Hosea 11:5; 12:6; 14:1–2
  e. Joel 2:12–13
  f. Zechariah 1:3–4
  g. Malachi 3:7

What does John's message have in common with the message of the Old Testament prophets? Where does it differ?

3. Read what God said concerning Jesus in Matthew 3:17, and compare this with the beginning of the Servant Song in Isaiah 42:1 and with Psalm 2:7. If Matthew 3:17 echoes these Old Testament texts, what does God's pronouncement after the baptism say about Jesus?

DISCUSSION GUIDE

1. In the first century, John declared that "the kingdom of heaven is at hand!" (Matt. 3:2). This and other passages speak of the nearness or presence of the kingdom. Elsewhere in Matthew, there are passages that speak of the kingdom as something still future (e.g., Matt. 6:10). Some theologians speak of the kingdom as something that has *already* been inaugurated at Christ's first coming but is *not yet* consummated. Does this already–not yet concept help explain these passages in Matthew? Why or why not?

2. What does John mean when he tells the Pharisees and Sadducees that God is able to raise up children for Abraham from stones (Matt. 3:9)?

3. Why is the active obedience of Christ as important as the passive obedience of Christ for our salvation?

APPLICATION

1. Those who have placed their faith in Christ have been baptized with water and with the Spirit. Remind yourself daily of the results of your baptism.

2. Do not grow weary in praying, "Thy kingdom come." Christ's kingdom has been inaugurated. He is seated at the right hand of God. He is presently putting all enemies under His feet, but the kingdom will not be consummated until His second coming. Thank God for our anointed King.

SUGGESTED READING FOR FURTHER STUDY

Blomberg, Craig. *Jesus and the Gospels,* pp. 221–22.

France, R. T. *The Gospel of Matthew,* pp. 96–124.

Keener, Craig. *A Commentary on the Gospel of Matthew,* pp. 116–35.

Lane, William L. *The Gospel according to Mark,* pp. 39–58.

Mathison, Keith A. *From Age to Age,* pp. 347–51.

Ridderbos, Herman. *The Gospel of John,* pp. 69–78.

Strauss, Mark L. *Four Portraits, One Jesus,* pp. 425–30.

Warrington, Keith. *Discovering Jesus in the New Testament,* pp. 9–12.

5

TEMPTATION

WHEN JESUS WAS BAPTIZED, the Holy Spirit descended on Him in the form of a dove, anointing Him for His ministry (Luke 3:22). However, the first thing the Spirit directed Him to do was not to preach, heal, or call disciples. Rather, the Spirit led Jesus into the wilderness so that He might be tempted by Satan (4:1–2).

Why did the Spirit want Jesus to be exposed to the unbridled assault of the Devil? I think the New Testament makes it clear that Jesus was called to be the last Adam or the new Adam so He might accomplish what the first Adam failed to accomplish. Of course, the major failure of the first Adam was his response to temptation.

The Apostle Paul wrote:

Therefore, just as through one man sin entered the world, and death through sin, and thus death spread to all men, because all sinned—(For until the law sin was in the world, but sin is not imputed when there is no law. Nevertheless death reigned from Adam to Moses, even over those who had not sinned according to the likeness of the transgression of Adam, who is a type of Him who was to come. But the free gift is not like the offense. For if by the one man's offense many died, much more the grace of God and the gift by the grace of the one Man, Jesus Christ, abounded to many….)

Therefore, as through one man's offense judgment came to all men, resulting in condemnation, even so through one Man's righteous act the free gift came to all men, resulting in justification of life. For as by one man's disobedience many were made sinners, so also by one Man's obedience many will be made righteous. (Rom. 5:12–15, 18–19)

Paul here compared and contrasted the first Adam and his failure to meet the terms of his probation under the attack of Satan, and the successful obedience of the last Adam, Jesus, who endured a similar temptation.

The two tests were of the same kind in some degrees, but in other ways, the terms of the temptation of Jesus differed radically from those that were imposed on Adam. Think first about the places where the two temptations took place. In the case of the first Adam, the temptation came while he and Eve were enjoying the pleasures of the garden of Eden, which we often refer to as Paradise. However, the place where the Spirit drove Jesus to be tempted could hardly be called Paradise. It was the desolate Judean wilderness, one of the most ominous and foreboding deserts anywhere in this world. It is said that the only inhabitants of the Judean wilderness are snakes and scorpions—even wildlife refuses to live in this place of desolation.

When Adam was exposed to the temptation of the Serpent, he was in the company of his wife, whom God had given to him by special creation to be his helpmate. Jesus, however, went into the wilderness in absolute solitude. It was the state of loneliness that received God's first malediction at creation. After He created everything, He pronounced it good with a benediction (Gen. 1:31). The first thing He said was *not* good was Adam's solitude. He said, "It is not good that man should be alone" (2:18). When we want to punish criminals or prisoners of war harshly, we send them into the state of solitary confinement, where they are cut off from ordinary human interaction and friendship. So it was with Jesus; He was driven into the wilderness to face temptation completely alone.

Furthermore, Adam was tempted in what could be described as a gourmet restaurant. In the lush environs of Eden, there were trees bearing all kinds of fruit that were wonderful to eat, and Adam and Eve were given the freedom to choose from any of those fruit-bearing trees to satisfy their hunger, with the single exception of the Tree of Knowledge of Good and Evil. Jesus' test came in the context of a forty-day fast in a harsh wilderness. So, while the first Adam was tested when his belly was full, the new Adam was tested when He was literally starving.

There is one more difference that I think needs to be mentioned. When Adam was tempted, there was no customary practice of sin. Sin was unknown before Adam and Eve committed it. But when Jesus was tested, there was nothing more commonplace in His world than the presence of sin. Why is that significant? One of the major factors that undermine our resolve to be righteous is that everyone around us sins. Therefore, we think it is no problem if we sin as well. Jesus had to act against the commonplace practice of human beings while He was undergoing these tests.

A SIMILAR POINT OF ATTACK

Despite these differences, there were similarities between the two temptations. First and foremost, Satan's point of attack against Adam and against Jesus was virtually the same. Consider the way in which the Serpent attacked Adam through Eve. He was said to be "more cunning than any beast of the field" (Gen. 3:1a). When he came against Eve, he came with a temptation clothed in subtlety. He asked what seemed to be a very simple question: "Has God indeed said, 'You shall not eat of every tree of the garden'?" (v. 1b). Had God said that? On the contrary, as Eve corrected the Serpent, "We may eat the fruit of the trees of the garden; but of the fruit of the tree which is in the midst of the garden, God has said, 'You shall not eat it, nor shall you touch it, lest you die'" (vv. 2–3). Eve told him, "No, God said, 'Of all of the trees of the garden you may freely eat,' but then He put one tree off limits, and said we are not allowed to eat from it, because if we do, we will surely die."

The Serpent tried to get Eve to think like a modern teenager. Imagine a teen who asks her parents on Monday night, "May I hang out at my friend's house tonight?" The parents give permission. The next night the teenager asks, "Can I borrow the car?" and again the parents agree. The next night the teen wants to go to a movie, the next night she needs to go shopping, and the next night she wants to go to a party after the high school football game. In each case, the parents agree. On the sixth night, Saturday night, the teenager requests permission to go with friends to the mall, but in this instance, the parents do not give permission. What is the teenager's response? "You never let me do anything." The parents may say yes many times, but if they say no just once, they are accused of *never* letting the teen do *anything*.

That scenario may be a bit clichéd, but it is not too different from the viewpoint Satan wanted Eve to adopt. The Serpent knew very well that God had not said that Adam and Eve could not eat from the trees of the garden, but by suggesting it, he caused her to focus on the restriction rather than the freedom. He suggested that if the man and the woman were not autonomous, if they were not totally free to choose whatever they wanted to choose, if any restriction had been placed on them by their Creator, then they were not really free, and He might just as well have said, "You cannot eat from any of the trees."

Then Satan moved from this subtle hint to a direct contradiction. After Eve set the record straight, Satan said, "You will not surely die. For God knows that in the day you eat of it your eyes will be opened, and you will be like God, knowing good and evil" (vv. 4–5). His point of attack was the trustworthiness, authority, and truth of the Word of God.

Theologian Emil Brunner once made the comment that the hallmark of truth is contradiction. That has always disturbed me, because if it is true that contradiction is the hallmark of truth, how can we discern the difference between godliness and ungodliness, between righteousness and unrighteousness, between obedience and disobedience?

I can imagine Satan using this argument, saying, "Yes, I know that I am contradicting God when I say that you will not die if you eat from the Tree of Knowledge of Good and Evil. However, you must remember, contradiction is the hallmark of truth. If God is a God of truth, I have just uttered the very hallmark of it, namely, the contradiction." If contradiction is the hallmark of truth, not only was Eve allowed to follow the suggestion of Satan, but it was imperative for her to do so. That is how distorted and twisted we can get in our thinking. In truth, contradiction is the hallmark of the lie. The essence of Satan's test was an assault on the truthfulness of God with a contradiction.

SEEKING TO UNDERMINE GOD'S WORD

Now notice how the temptation of Jesus unfolded. Satan came to Him after His fast of forty days and forty nights, when He was very hungry. When the tempter came to Him, he said, "If You are the Son of God, command that these stones become bread" (Matt. 4:3). Notice the subtle suggestion: "*If* You are the Son of God, You should turn these stones into bread. If You are the Son of God, why are You starving to death here in the wilderness? You have the power to relieve Your hunger, don't You?" Remember, the last words Jesus heard before He went into the wilderness, after He was baptized and the Spirit descended on Him, were the words of God the Father speaking audibly from heaven and saying, "This is My beloved Son, in whom I am well pleased" (Matt. 3:17). He had just heard the Father publicly declare Him to be the Son of God. But then the Serpent came and challenged the very affirmation the Father had made.

How did Jesus respond to the Devil's temptation? He replied, "It is written, 'Man shall not live by bread alone, but by every word that proceeds from the mouth of God'" (Matt. 4:4, citing Deut. 8:3). He did not defend His identity as the Son of God. He simply cited the Word of God. Obedience to the will of the Father expressed in the Word of God was more important to Him than satisfying His hunger. I firmly believe He was willing to starve to death rather than deny the truthfulness of His Father's Word.

Then Satan took Him to Jerusalem and set Him on the pinnacle of the temple. He said, "If You are the Son of God, throw Yourself down. For it is written: 'He shall give His angels charge over you,' and, 'In their hands they shall bear you up, lest you dash your foot against a stone'" (Matt. 4:6). It was as if Satan was saying: "If you are going to quote Scripture at me, Jesus, let's test it. You think the Scriptures cannot be broken. You think that Your Father's Word is true. Well, we can prove it. All You have to do is jump from the pinnacle of the temple and, if the Word of God is true, the angels will catch You. If You really believe that the Word of God is true, You have nothing to worry about."

What did Jesus reply? Again, He went to Scripture: "It is written again, 'You shall not tempt the LORD your God'" (Matt. 4:7, citing Deut. 6:16). Jesus was saying that a cardinal rule of biblical interpretation is that one portion is not to be set against another portion. If He agreed to Satan's suggestion that He jump off the temple, He would be putting the Father to the test. That He refused to do. He knew the angels had charge over Him. He did not need to see physical proof to believe the Word of God.

Finally, Satan took Jesus up to a high mountain and showed Him all the kingdoms of the world. Then he said, "All these things I will give You if You will fall down and worship me" (Matt. 4:9). He offered Jesus all the authority and glory the world has to give. He portrayed the price as small. He might have said: "All You have to do is make a small genuflection. No one will see it. Just bow to me just once and it's all Yours. You will inherit the world without suffering, without humiliation, without pain, without crucifixion." But Jesus said to him: "Away with you, Satan! For it is written, 'You shall worship the LORD your God, and Him only you shall serve'" (Matt. 4:10, citing Deut. 6:13).

Three times the assault came. Three times the assault was directed against the trustworthiness of the Word of God. With every subtlety at his disposal, using even the words of Scripture itself, Satan tried to seduce Jesus to go against the Word of God. But Jesus refused. He drove the Serpent from the wilderness.

So, Satan left Jesus for the moment, "until an opportune time" (Luke 4:13). This was not the end. Throughout His life, Jesus experienced Satan continually coming against Him to try to get Him to go a different way. The temptation often came from His best friends. As soon as He told them He had to go to Jerusalem to suffer, Peter said, "Far be it from You, Lord; this shall not happen to You!" (Matt. 16:22). What did Jesus say? He turned to Peter and said vehemently: "Get behind Me, Satan! You are an offense to Me, for you are not mindful of the things of God, but the things of men" (v. 23).

Jesus obeyed at every point in the temptation. Then, when the Serpent left Him, "angels came and ministered to Him" (Matt. 4:11). They helped Him in His hunger, in His loneliness, and in His pain. But they did not arrive at the last second, like the cavalry in an old Western movie. They were there the whole time. Jesus knew the Father had given the angels charge over Him. Jesus trusted in the truth of His Father's Word.

CHAPTER 5

STUDY GUIDE

INTRODUCTION

Immediately after His baptism, Jesus was driven into the wilderness to be tempted by the Devil. We are reminded here not only of Israel's testing in the wilderness, but also of the original test—the temptation of Adam. In this chapter, Dr. R. C. Sproul compares and contrasts the temptations of the first Adam and the second Adam, explaining how the results of each rested on whether trust was placed in the Word of God.

LEARNING OBJECTIVES

1. To be able to explain the process by which the Serpent was able to tempt Adam and Eve to distrust the Word of God.
2. To be able to explain the similarities and differences between the temptations of Adam and Jesus.

QUOTATIONS

"Yea, hath God said …?"

—Satan (Gen. 3:1 KJV)

"It is written …"

—Jesus (Matt. 4:4)

OUTLINE

I. Introduction

 A. Following Jesus' baptism, the very first thing the Spirit directed Jesus to do was to go into the wilderness to be tempted for forty days.

 B. The reason He had to be tempted was because part of His essential work was to be the second Adam.

C. Two important passages presenting Christ as the second Adam:
1. Romans 5:12–19
2. 1 Corinthians 15:21–22, 45–49

II. The Differences between Adam's Temptation and Jesus' Temptation

A. Location
1. The first Adam was tempted in Paradise.
2. The second Adam was tempted in a desolate wilderness.

B. Companionship
1. The first Adam was tempted while together with Eve.
2. The second Adam was tempted while in absolute solitude.

C. Food
1. The first Adam was tempted while able to eat all kinds of food.
2. The second Adam was tempted during a forty-day fast.

D. Sin
1. The first Adam was tempted before there was any customary practice of sin.
2. The second Adam was tempted when there was nothing more commonplace than the practice of sin.

III. The Similarities between Adam's Temptation and Jesus' Temptation

A. The Temptation of Adam

1. The Serpent's temptation of Eve began with the subtle question "Has God indeed said …?" (Gen. 3:1).

2. Satan questioned the Word of God.

3. Eve informed the Serpent that God had not said what was suggested.

4. The Serpent then moved to a lie, contradicting God's Word directly.

5. The point of attack was the trustworthiness, authority, and truth of the Word of God.

B. The Temptation of Jesus

1. Satan attacked Jesus at the end of a forty-day fast.

2. He said, "If You are the Son of God …"

3. This questioned the truthfulness of the words God spoke following Jesus' baptism.

4. Jesus responded by appealing to the Word of God.

5. Satan then attacked Jesus by quoting Scripture.

6. Jesus responded by denying Satan's interpretation of Scripture, an interpretation that set one part of Scripture against another part.

7. Finally Satan promised Jesus that He would be given all the kingdoms of the world if He would only worship Satan.

8. Again, Jesus responded by appealing to the written Word of God.

BIBLE STUDY

1. All three of Jesus' responses to Satan's temptations are quotations taken from Deuteronomy 6–8. These chapters of Deuteronomy warn Israel not to forget God as they did during the previous generation. Read Deuteronomy 6–8. How does Jesus recapitulate Israel's experience in the wilderness? What does this indicate about the nature of Jesus' ministry?

2. Read the account of the Serpent's temptation of Adam and Eve in Genesis 3:1–6 and compare it with the accounts of the temptation in Matthew, Mark, and Luke. What do the similarities indicate about the nature of Jesus' ministry?

3. Read Romans 5:12–19 and 1 Corinthians 15:21–49. What important theological doctrines did Paul rest on the comparison between Adam and Jesus?

DISCUSSION GUIDE

1. Adam, Israel, and Jesus are all referred to at some point in Scripture as God's "son" (e.g., Luke 3:38; Hosea 11:1; Matt. 3:17). Does this help us understand why Jesus' temptation shows similarities to the testing of both Adam and Israel? Why or why not?

2. Matthew in particular drew comparisons between Jesus and Israel throughout the first chapters of his gospel. The genealogy presents Jesus as the culmination of Israel's history. The flight to and return from Egypt indicates that the long-awaited new exodus has begun. The slaughter of the children portrays Jesus as a new Moses. The forty-day testing in the wilderness is reminiscent of Israel's forty-year time of wilderness testing, and the Sermon on the Mount reminds us of the giving of the law on Mount Sinai. If Jesus is in some sense recapitulating Israel's history, how might this help us better understand both the Old and the New Testaments?

APPLICATION

1. Are you surprised when God allows you to experience times of extreme difficulty, testing, and temptation? Consider again that the Son of God Himself experienced such testing. Be encouraged, for He does not allow us to be tested beyond what we can handle.

2. Meditate on Matthew 4:1–11 today. Consider the fact that Satan's temptations are not always overt and obvious but sometimes very subtle. Guard your heart in dependence on the grace of God to withstand the assaults of the Enemy when they come.

3. Take the time to study the portion of Scripture Jesus used in His response to Satan, Deuteronomy 6–8. Memorize it if you are able.

SUGGESTED READING FOR FURTHER STUDY

Blomberg, Craig. *Jesus and the Gospels,* pp. 222–24.

France, R. T. *The Gospel of Matthew,* pp. 124–36.

Keener, Craig. *A Commentary on the Gospel of Matthew,* pp. 136–44.

Lane, William L. *The Gospel according to Mark,* pp. 59–62.

Mathison, Keith A. *From Age to Age,* p. 350.

Morris, Leon. *The Gospel according to Matthew,* pp. 69–79.

Strauss, Mark L. *Four Portraits, One Jesus,* pp. 430–32.

Warrington, Keith. *Discovering Jesus in the New Testament,* pp. 12–14.

6

TRANSFIGURATION

THE TRANSFIGURATION OF JESUS took place near the end of His ministry, whereas His temptation, which we examined in the previous chapter, happened near the beginning. Thus, we make a rather significant leap in time from the previous chapter to this one. Does that mean that everything between His temptation and transfiguration was meaningless? Of course not. During most of His earthly ministry, Jesus was occupied with preaching, teaching about the coming of the kingdom of God, and healing the sick (and, in some cases, raising the dead). But one of His chief responsibilities in His incarnation was to show forth the very glory of God, and that is what happened in an especially glorious way before a small audience of three men, Peter, James, and John, on the Mount of Transfiguration.

I love to consider the transfiguration of Jesus. If I had the opportunity to go back in time and be an eyewitness of any event in Jesus' life, I would most want to see the resurrection. Next to that, however, the one event of His life that I would want to see more than anything else would be His transfiguration, because that episode not only gives us information about Jesus, but also communicates to us something of vital importance to His ministry.

Matthew's account of this event reads:

> Now after six days Jesus took Peter, James, and John his brother, led them up on a high mountain by themselves; and He was transfigured before them. His face shone like the sun, and His clothes became as white as the light. And behold, Moses and Elijah appeared to them, talking with Him. Then Peter answered and said to Jesus, "Lord, it is good for us to be here; if You wish, let us make here three tabernacles: one for You, one for Moses, and one for Elijah."
>
> While he was still speaking, behold, a bright cloud overshadowed them; and suddenly a voice came out of the cloud, saying, "This is My beloved Son, in whom I am well pleased. Hear Him!" And when the disciples heard it, they fell on their faces and were greatly afraid. But Jesus came and touched them and said, "Arise, do not be afraid." When they had lifted up their eyes, they saw no one but Jesus only. (17:1–8)

As Jesus was winding up His public ministry and setting His face to go to Jerusalem, knowing full well the suffering and death that awaited Him there, He went apart to a high mountain with Peter, James, and John. Matthew tells us that while they were on the mountain, Jesus was "transfigured" before the three disciples' eyes. What does this mean? The word that is translated "transfigured" is a form of the Greek verb *metamorphoo,* which means "to change into another form." The English word *metamorphosis* comes directly from this Greek word. We speak of metamorphosis when we see a caterpillar spinning a cocoon and later emerging as a beautiful butterfly. So, transfiguration is fundamentally an alteration, a change of the outward form. That is what happened to Jesus on the top of the mountain.

A SHINING FACE

Matthew says, "His face shone like the sun" (17:2a). His face, His countenance, began to shine with an intensity equal to that of the sun. When I read that description, I am reminded of how Moses pleaded with God for the *visio Dei,* the grand vision of God Himself. Moses had been an eyewitness of the bush that burned but was not consumed (Exod. 3). He had been an eyewitness of Israel's miraculous deliverance from the chariots of Egypt at the Red Sea (Exod. 14). But he wanted more, so he asked God, "Please, show me Your glory." God replied:

> I will make all My goodness pass before you, and I will
> proclaim the name of the LORD before you…. [But]
> you cannot see My face; for no man shall see Me, and
> live…. Here is a place by Me, and you shall stand on
> the rock. So it shall be, while My glory passes by, that
> I will put you in the cleft of the rock, and will cover
> you with My hand while I pass by. Then I will take
> away My hand, and you shall see My back; but My
> face shall not be seen. (Exod. 33:18–23)

God did as He promised and moved past Moses while Moses
was hidden in a niche in the rock (Exod. 33:21–23; 34:5–7). All
Moses saw was a backward glance of the glory of God, but when he
came down from Mount Sinai, his face shone with such intensity
that he had to cover it, for the people of Israel were terrified by what
they saw (Exod. 34:29–35).

Of course, the glory of God that radiated in such a brilliant way
from the face of Moses was a reflected glory, an echo of God's own
glory. It did not come from Moses himself. It came from the back
of God. But on the Mount of Transfiguration, Jesus did not simply
reflect the glory of God. The brilliant light that shone from His face
emanated from within Him. Its origin was in His own being, His
own divine nature.

The author of Hebrews described Jesus as "the brightness of
[God's] glory and the express image of His person" (1:3a). God the
Father manifested Himself throughout biblical history in the blind-
ing glory of the *shekinah* cloud. When Solomon built the temple

in Jerusalem and brought the ark of the covenant into it, "it came to pass, when the priests came out of the holy place, that the cloud filled the house of the LORD, so that the priests could not continue ministering because of the cloud; for the glory of the LORD filled the house of the LORD" (1 Kings 8:10–11). This was the same glory that shone forth from Jesus on the mountain.

Paul witnessed the glory of Christ on the road to Damascus as he was moving rapidly to carry out his work of persecution against Christ and His church: "As he journeyed he came near Damascus, and suddenly a light shone around him from heaven. Then he fell to the ground, and heard a voice saying to him, 'Saul, Saul, why are you persecuting Me?' And he said, 'Who are You, Lord?' Then the Lord said, 'I am Jesus, whom you are persecuting'" (Acts 9:3–5a). A glorious light marked Paul's encounter with Jesus on the road to Damascus, and he was temporarily blinded. Later, he described this light as "a light from heaven, brighter than the sun" (Acts 26:13).

The book of Revelation tells us about the New Jerusalem, the city of God that will be the home of God's people in the new earth. It says: "The city had no need of the sun or of the moon to shine in it, for the glory of God illuminated it. The Lamb is its light…. Its gates shall not be shut at all by day (there shall be no night there)" (21:23, 25). John speaks of a place with no sun and no moon, for there is no need of them. There is a greater light there. The glory of God illumines the city, and the Lamb is its light, such that there is no night. When the radiance of God's glory is unveiled, all is light, and darkness must flee away.

Peter, James, and John experienced a taste of this on the Mount of Transfiguration as Jesus revealed His true glory to them. It was an experience they never forgot. In the prologue of his gospel, John wrote, "In the beginning was the Word, and the Word was with God, and the Word was God.... And the Word became flesh and dwelt among us, and we beheld His glory, the glory as of the only begotten of the Father, full of grace and truth" (John 1:1, 14). The disciples saw the unveiled glory of the only begotten Son of God.

CLOTHING OF PURE WHITE

Matthew also notes, "His clothes became as white as the light" (17:2b). Mark says His clothes became "exceedingly white, like snow, such as no launderer on earth can whiten them" (9:3). His garments were absolutely white, without a fleck of gray, a single blemish, or the most microscopic stain.

When I preach on this passage, I always point to a child somewhere in the congregation and ask a simple question: "What color is a lemon?" The child always gets the answer right and says, "A lemon is yellow." I then follow up with a deeper question: "What color is a lemon in the dark?" With that, we move into the realm of the age-old philosophical inquiry about primary and secondary qualities. Nearly everyone assumes that a lemon remains yellow when the lights go out. However, color is not a primary quality; it is a secondary quality. It is not something that inheres inside of an object. The color we experience in this world is the result of the action of light, for all the hues of the rainbow are found in the pure light of the sun. In the absence of light, all we perceive is black. But when all the colors are mixed in the purity of light, we see absolute white. Thus, the fact that Jesus' clothes were pure white tells us something about the light that was emanating from Him.

My favorite novel is Herman Melville's *Moby Dick*. My favorite chapter in *Moby Dick* is titled "The Whiteness of the Whale." In that chapter, Melville explores the many ways in which whiteness is a symbol in human experience: the symbol of virginity and purity, the mark of the spectral quality of a ghost, and so on. In writing his novel about the hunt for a great whale, Melville chose to make the whale an albino as a symbol for God. The whale's whiteness simultaneously displays God's glory, power, and majesty, but it also portrays a shroud behind which His identity is hidden. The whale embodies all that is symbolized by whiteness—that which is pure, excellent, and mysterious, but also terrifying, ghastly, and horrible—so he carries the traits that are found in the fullness of the perfection of God.

A CLOUD AND A VOICE

Peter, James, and John saw still more. Matthew wrote, "And behold, Moses and Elijah appeared to them, talking with Him" (17:3). Moses and Elijah represent the Law and the Prophets coming together, talking to the Messiah about His destiny, about the task that lay before Him. In order to fulfill the Law and the Prophets, Jesus had to suffer and die.

This sight was more than Peter could handle. He began babbling: "Lord, it is good for us to be here; if You wish, let us make here three tabernacles: one for You, one for Moses, and one for Elijah" (v. 4). It seems that Peter was enraptured and wanted to remain on the mountain, basking in this "mountaintop" spiritual experience.

While he was still speaking this nonsense, "behold, a bright cloud overshadowed them; and suddenly a voice came out of the cloud, saying, 'This is My beloved Son, in whom I am well pleased. Hear Him!'" (v. 5). The disciples' experience on the Mount of Transfiguration was not just visual; it was aural, too. They heard the voice of the Father speaking from heaven. The content of the Father's words was significant. He not only stated who Jesus was and affirmed His pleasure in Him, just as He did at Jesus' baptism (Matt. 3:17), but also commanded the disciples to hear what Jesus had to say. That is precisely what the Father would say to us were He to speak from heaven today.

Not surprisingly, "when the disciples heard it, they fell on their faces and were greatly afraid. But Jesus came and touched them and said, 'Arise, and do not be afraid'" (vv. 6–7). When they lifted their eyes, Moses and Elijah were gone. The metamorphosis was over, and they saw Jesus as they had seen Him all the days of His earthly ministry (v. 8).

I would have loved to have seen the transfiguration. By God's grace, however, I will see it someday, and I can't wait. All believers will see it because heaven will be a perpetual Mount of Transfiguration. There will be no more concealment, but the white, brilliant light of the glory of God and of His Lamb will be there for our vision every moment.

CHAPTER 6

STUDY GUIDE

INTRODUCTION

At the beginning of the gospel of John, the Apostle declared, "And the Word became flesh and dwelt among us, and we beheld His glory" (1:14). It is very likely that John was referring here to the transfiguration of Christ, that moment when the glory theretofore concealed was revealed to Jesus' closest disciples. In this chapter, Dr. R. C. Sproul looks at the account of the transfiguration, explaining its significance in the ministry of Christ.

LEARNING OBJECTIVES

1. To be able to place the transfiguration in the context of previous revelations of the glory of Christ.
2. To be able to explain the significance of the transfiguration in the life and work of Christ.

QUOTATIONS

One of the greatest privileges and advancements of believers, both in this world, and unto eternity, consists in their beholding the glory of Christ.

—John Owen, *The Glorious Mystery of the Person of Christ, God and Man*

The transfiguration is a dramatic indication of the resplendent glory which belongs to Jesus as God's unique Son. As a revelation of the concealed splendor of the Son of Man, the event points forward to the advent ... when Jesus' status as the eschatological Judge will be manifested to the world. The episode provides a personal and preliminary revelation that he whom the disciples follow on a way marked by suffering and humiliation is the Son of Man whose total ministry has cosmic implications.

—William Lane, *The Gospel according to Mark*

OUTLINE

I. Introduction

    A. Jesus' transfiguration communicated something of vital importance.

    B. One of His chief responsibilities was to manifest the glory of God.

II. The Transfiguration

    A. Matthew's account of the transfiguration is found in chapter 17 of his gospel.

    B. There was a general progression in the life of Jesus that moved from humiliation to exaltation.

    C. For the most part, the deity that Christ shared with the Father and Holy Spirit was cloaked.

    D. As Jesus began His final trek to Jerusalem, He went to a high mountain with Peter, James, and John where He was transfigured before their eyes.

    E. The word *transfiguration* comes from the Greek word *metamorphoo*.

    F. We get the English word *metamorphosis* from this Greek word.

III. Jesus' Face

    A. Matthew says that Jesus' face shone like the sun.

    B. This reminds us of what happened to Moses after he caught a glimpse of God's glory (Exod. 34:29–33).

    C. After God revealed Himself to Moses, his face shone, and he had to veil himself before the people of Israel.

    D. Moses shone with the reflected light of God's glory, but Jesus shone with light that emanated from within Himself.

    E. Paul saw this glory on the road to Damascus.

    F. This glory is so bright that there will be no need for sunlight in the new heavens and new earth.

IV. Jesus' Clothes

    A. Matthew also tells us that Jesus' clothes became white as light.

    B. There was not a single blemish or stain.

    C. The absence of all color is blackness.

    D. The reflection of all color is absolute white.

    E. Herman Melville's *Moby Dick* contains a chapter titled "The Whiteness of the Whale," which portrays the whale as a symbol for God.

V. The Voice of God

A. As Jesus was transfigured, Moses and Elijah joined Him on the mountain.

B. Moses represented the Law, while Elijah represented the Prophets.

C. Peter offered to make three tents: one for Jesus, one for Moses, and one for Elijah.

D. While Peter was still speaking, a cloud overshadowed them, and a voice came from the cloud.

E. They heard the voice say, "This is My beloved Son, in whom I am well pleased. Hear Him!"

BIBLE STUDY

1. Numerous commentators have noted apparent parallels between the Sinai account in Exodus and the transfiguration account in the Gospels (Matt. 17:1–8; Mark 9:2–8; Luke 9:28–36). The following are some of the possible parallels:

a. Both involve a high mountain (cf. Exod. 24:12, 15–18).

b. In both, a cloud descends on the mountain (cf. Exod. 24:15–18).

c. In both, God speaks from the cloud (cf. Exod. 24:16).

d. The central figure in both accounts becomes radiant (cf. Exod. 34:29–35).

e. In both accounts, the events are said to begin after six days (cf. Exod. 24:16).

If the transfiguration was intended to echo the Sinai account, what would its main point be?

2. The transfiguration account speaks of a "bright cloud" (Matt. 17:5 ESV). Given texts such as Exodus 24:15–18 and 40:34–38, how should we understand this cloud that descends on the mountain at the transfiguration?

3. Read Deuteronomy 18:15. How does Matthew 17:5 allude to this verse? Granted that Matthew has Deuteronomy 18 in mind, what are we being told about Jesus?

4. Matthew 17:6 and 27:54 are the only two places where Matthew uses the Greek phrase *ephobethesan sphodra,* which has to do with being terrified or filled with fear. Are there any other similarities between the transfiguration account and the crucifixion account?

DISCUSSION GUIDE

1. All three accounts of the transfiguration are preceded by an enigmatic prophecy made a week earlier in which Christ said,

"Truly, I say to you, there are some standing here who will not taste death until they see the Son of Man coming in his kingdom" (Matt. 16:28 ESV; cf. Mark 9:1; Luke 9:27). Some commentators and theologians argue that the transfiguration is the fulfillment of this prophecy. Is this likely? Why or why not?

2. Matthew in particular tends to portray Jesus in terms of a "new Moses." How does the account of the transfiguration contribute to this understanding of Christ? What are the similarities and differences between Moses and Jesus?

3. Why do you think Jesus revealed His glory to only three of the disciples rather than to all of them?

APPLICATION

1. Take time this week to read and meditate on 2 Corinthians 3:18, which says that we all beholding the glory of the Lord are being transformed into the same image from one degree of glory to another.

2. We hear the Word of the Lord preached weekly. Do you listen to Him? If not, resolve to do so beginning today.

SUGGESTED READING FOR FURTHER STUDY

Allison, Dale C. *The New Moses,* pp. 243–48.

Davies, W. D., and D. C. Allison. *Matthew 8–18,* pp. 684–709.

Edwards, James R. *The Gospel according to Mark,* pp. 261–71.

France, R. T. *Matthew: Evangelist and Teacher,* pp. 186–89.

Macleod, Donald. *The Person of Christ,* pp. 101–7.

7

TRIUMPHAL
ENTRY

THE JOY OF THE disciples who witnessed the glory of Jesus on the Mount of Transfiguration rapidly turned to despair when Jesus announced to them that they were going to Jerusalem, where He would be betrayed and would undergo suffering and death. The disciples were "exceedingly sorrowful" when they heard this (Matt. 17:23). Yet, this march to Jerusalem set up one of the most joyous moments of Jesus' ministry.

Matthew recounts what happened when Jesus and His disciples reached Jerusalem:

Now when they drew near Jerusalem, and came to

Bethphage, at the Mount of Olives, then Jesus sent two disciples, saying to them, "Go into the village opposite you, and immediately you will find a donkey tied, and a colt with her. Loose them and bring them to Me. And if anyone says anything to you, you shall say, 'The Lord has need of them,' and immediately he will send them."

All this was done that it might be fulfilled which was spoken by the prophet, saying: "Tell the daughter of Zion, 'Behold, your King is coming to you, lowly, and sitting on a donkey, a colt, the foal of a donkey.'"

So the disciples went and did as Jesus commanded them. They brought the donkey and the colt, laid their clothes on them, and set Him on them. And a very great multitude spread their clothes on the road; others cut down branches from the trees and spread them on the road. Then the multitudes who went before and those who followed cried out, saying, "Hosanna to the Son of David! 'Blessed is He who comes in the name of the LORD!' Hosanna in the highest!" And when He had come into Jerusalem, all the city was moved, saying, "Who is this?" So the multitudes said, "This is Jesus, the prophet from Nazareth of Galilee." (21:1–11)

This is the account of that event in biblical history known as the triumphal entry of Jesus. One of the interesting aspects of this account is that two distinct Jewish offices are mentioned: the office of king and the office of prophet.

When Jesus entered the city, He came as royalty. His mode of transportation was lowly, to be sure. Nevertheless, He consciously fulfilled the Old Testament announcement through the prophet Zechariah that the King of the Jews would come to Jerusalem riding on a donkey.

By entering Jerusalem in this way, and by allowing the crowds to laud Him, Jesus took the wraps off His most carefully guarded secret. Nearly every time there was mention during Jesus' earthly ministry about His identity as the Messiah, He instructed His disciples to tell no one. We call this "the messianic secret." We have to guess as to why Jesus insisted on secrecy regarding His messianic vocation, and the best guess is that He understood that the people had an incorrect understanding of what the Messiah would do. The popular hope and expectation was that the Messiah would be a great warrior who would overthrow the oppression of the Roman Empire and liberate the people of Israel.

But Jesus' understanding of the mission of the Messiah was much deeper, taking into account all the strands of expectation in Old Testament prophecy. The most important strand of all, seen most clearly in the book of Isaiah (52–53), showed that the Messiah would be a lowly servant who would suffer. However, that picture was not popular, so Jesus kept His identity under wraps until He came to Jerusalem for the last time. There, as He made His triumphal entry, the cloak of concealment was removed, and Jesus, clearly fulfilling Old Testament prophecy, came into the city in a joyous procession indicating His position of royalty.

But notice that when the people of Jerusalem asked, "Who is this?" one of the answers that was given was, "This is Jesus, the prophet from Nazareth of Galilee." Thus, we see another element of Jesus' work mentioned in this passage—His work as a prophet.

Of course, the New Testament teaches that Jesus fulfills not just two offices but three. In theology, we call those three offices the *munus triplex,* the threefold office of Jesus. They include—in addition to king and prophet—the office of priest. He fulfilled all three offices in His person and in His work. It is helpful to our understanding of Jesus' mission to distinguish among these three offices.

PROPHETS, PRIESTS, AND KINGS

All three offices—prophet, priest, and king—were performed by some kind of mediator. The Scriptures emphasize Christ's uniqueness as the only Mediator between humanity and God, but that is not to exclude the lower forms of mediatorial service that functioned in Old Testament days in the offices of the prophet, the priest, and the king. They, too, were mediators because, in some way, each of them stood between the people and God.

The basic difference between the prophet and the priest was that the prophet was God's spokesman, whereas the priests carried out the normal duties of the religious organization of Israel. The prophet would preface his statements by saying, "Thus says the Lord," for the prophets were agents of revelation. God put His word in their mouths, so they served as the spokesmen for God to the people. The priests, on the other hand, served in a regular office, not a special, charismatically appointed office like that of the prophets. The two main functions they performed were the offering of sacrifices and the offering of prayers. Thus, the priest was the mediator for the people to God.

In the church today, the offices of prophet and priest have been combined. In the liturgy of a Protestant worship service, certain elements are priestly and others are prophetic. When the pastor prays for the people, he is engaged in a priestly activity. When he reads the Scriptures and preaches the sermon, he is engaged in a prophetic activity.

In New Testament categories, the supreme prophet of all time is Jesus. He did not just speak the Word of God during His time on earth; rather, He *is* the Word of God. When He speaks, He speaks with the full authority of the Father.

The chief difference between the Old Testament prophets and Jesus has to do with what I call the subjective and objective elements. The subjective element of prophecy was the prophet himself. The objective element was his message, which ultimately was concerned with the One who was to come, Jesus. By contrast, Jesus was both the subject and the object of prophecy. That is, most of the prophetic statements that He uttered were about Himself.

Those who want to reduce Christianity to a set of moral guidelines and restrict Jesus to the role of ethical teacher or moralist fail to observe that much of what Jesus said was about Himself. For instance, in the Beatitudes section of the Sermon on the Mount, the blessings find their fullest expression in Him and in His kingdom. Even in the Beatitudes, which so often are regarded as moral aphorisms, Jesus was making statements about His work in the kingdom of God.

The work of the priests also had subjective and objective dimensions. They had subjective involvement in the tasks they performed, but the object of their work was the sacrifices they offered on behalf of the people. But Jesus not only performed the work of a priest in offering a sacrifice, He Himself was the object, the sacrifice. All the sacrifices that were offered by the priests in the Old Testament were basically symbolic, mere shadows of the full and perfect sacrifice that was to be offered once and for all by Christ. We do not repeat animal sacrifices in the Christian church today because everything that the animal sacrifices pointed to was fulfilled in the perfect sacrifice of Jesus.

PRIESTHOOD AND KINGSHIP

The book of Hebrews deals with a key question regarding the offices of Christ: How can He be both a Priest and a King? The Old Testament prophets made it very clear that the Messiah would come from the Israelite tribe of Judah. The kingship of Israel had been given to Judah (Gen. 49:10), and God had promised that the Messiah would be Israel's perfect King, a ruler who would come from the loins of David and the line of Judah. The New Testament goes to great lengths to demonstrate that Jesus was of the tribe of Judah, and therefore was qualified to be King. However, He is also called a Priest. Yet, the priesthood was given to the line of Aaron of the tribe of Levi. How, then, could Jesus be both a Priest and a King? It would seem that if He was qualified to be the King by His lineage from Judah, He was not qualified to be a Priest.

The author of Hebrews explained that Jesus was a Priest, not of the order of Levi, but of the order of Melchizedek (Heb. 5:6, citing Ps. 110:4). He made the argument that the priestly order of Melchizedek was a higher order of priesthood than that of Levi (Heb. 7). The author of Hebrews reminded his readers of the strange, brief story found in Genesis 14, wherein Abraham met an enigmatic figure named Melchizedek. The name Melchizedek means "king of righteousness." Furthermore, he was the king of Salem, which means "peace." Thus, Melchizedek could be known as the "king of righteousness" and the "king of peace."

This Melchizedek blessed Abraham and received tithes from him. In Old Testament categories, the greater blessed the lesser, and the lesser paid tithes to the greater. The author of Hebrews pointed out that Levi, who was not yet born, would be a great-grandson of Abraham, making him lesser than Abraham. Logically, then, if Abraham was greater than Levi, and Melchizedek was greater than Abraham, then Melchizedek was greater than Levi, and Melchizedek's priesthood therefore was greater than Levi's. Thus, the priestly office that Jesus fulfills surpasses everything in the Old Testament Aaronic or Levitical priesthood.

The triumphal entry shows that Jesus also held the third office, the office of king. Looking again at the Old Testament economy, we see that the king of Israel was not autonomous. The king did not have supreme authority; rather, he was called to mediate the righteous rule of God to the people, and he was accountable to God for how he carried out his office. Later, the New Testament made it clear that *all* officials in government and authority are likewise subordinate to the authority of God and will be judged by God for how they carry out their office. But in ancient Israel, the kings lost sight of this truth and, particularly in the northern kingdom, sought supreme authority for themselves and flagrantly disobeyed the law of God.

However, the King who rode into Jerusalem that day on the back of a donkey was David's son and at the same time David's Lord (Luke 20:41–44). He fulfilled all of the Old Testament promises of the coming King who would restore the house of David and usher in the kingdom of God. To this King, God would give all authority in heaven and on earth, and His reign would be eternal. There would be no succession, no need for a son or daughter to assume His throne. He is the King of the Kings and the Lord of the Lords.

So, as Jesus rode into Jerusalem, He was on the cusp of the culmination of who He was and what He had come to do as the supreme Prophet, who would give the clearest revelation of God; the ultimate Priest, who would present the perfect sacrifice; and the almighty King, who would reign forever and ever.

CHAPTER 7

STUDY GUIDE

INTRODUCTION

When "the prophet Jesus, from Nazareth of Galilee" (Matt. 21:11 ESV) triumphantly entered Jerusalem, He did so in fulfillment of an Old Testament promise that Israel's King would come to the city riding a donkey. In this chapter, Dr. R. C. Sproul examines Jesus' three mediatorial offices, not only as our Prophet and King, but also as our High Priest.

LEARNING OBJECTIVES

1. To be able to explain Christ's role in the office of prophet.
2. To be able to explain Christ's role in the office of priest.
3. To be able to explain Christ's role in the office of king.

QUOTATIONS

> In Christ's God-to-humanity relation, he is a prophet; in his humanity-to-God relation he is a priest; in his headship over all humanity he is a king.
>
> —Herman Bavinck, *Reformed Dogmatics*

> It is by the exercise and discharge of the office of Christ—as the king, priest, and prophet of the church—that we are redeemed, sanctified, and saved. Thereby doth he immediately communicate all Gospel benefits unto us—give us an access unto God here by grace, and in glory hereafter; for he saves us, as he is the mediator between God and man.
>
> —John Owen, *The Person of Christ*

OUTLINE

I. Introduction

    A. The transfiguration was a moment of unsurpassed glory and joy for the disciples who beheld it.

    B. The joy turned to despair when Jesus reminded them that He was going to Jerusalem, where He would suffer and die.

II. The Triumphal Entry

    A. The account of the triumphal entry is found in Matthew 21.

    B. Why did Jesus stage such a grand entry?

    C. Matthew tells us He did it in order to fulfill Old Testament prophecy.

    D. In the account of the triumphal entry, two of Christ's offices are in view: prophet and king.

    E. Prior to this point in time Jesus did not want His disciples to tell anyone He was the Messiah.

    F. The people had an incorrect understanding of what the Messiah would do.

    G. The people expected a great warrior who would free them from Rome, but Christ was focused on the Messiah's role as a suffering servant.

    H. At His triumphal entry, He no longer concealed His identity.

III. The Offices of Christ

    A. All three offices are performed by some kind of mediator.

    B. Christ is the unique Mediator, but that does not mean lower forms of mediatorial service did not function in Old Testament times.

    C. What made them mediators was that they stood in some way between the people and God.

IV. The Prophet

    A. The supreme Prophet of all time is Jesus.

    B. Jesus does not simply speak the Word; He is the Word.

    C. The difference between Jesus and the rest of the prophets is that Jesus was both the subject and the object of prophecy.

    D. Most of the prophetic statements that Jesus made were about Himself.

V. The Priest

    A. Priests also had subjective and objective dimensions to their work.

    B. They were subjectively involved in making the offerings.

    C. Their principal task was to offer sacrifices on behalf of the people.

D. When Jesus offered the sacrifice, the sacrifice He offered was Himself.

E. All of the Old Testament sacrifices were symbolic and pointed to Christ.

F. Jesus' contemporaries couldn't understand how Jesus could be both priest and king because the king was to be from the tribe of Judah and priests were from the tribe of Levi.

G. Jesus was a priest in the order of Melchizedek, which is a higher order of priesthood than that of the Levites.

VI. The King

A. In the triumphal entry, the accent is on the office of king.

B. In the Old Testament economy, the king was not autonomous.

C. The king was subject to God's law and was supposed to mediate God's rule.

D. Jesus is the One who is both David's son and David's Lord.

E. Jesus fulfilled all of the Old Testament promises concerning the coming King.

F. To this King, God promised to give all authority in heaven and on earth.

BIBLE STUDY

1. Read Exodus 7:1 and Deuteronomy 18:18. What are the two elements involved in the function of a prophet? Hint: One element is passive; one is active.

2. What insight do the following texts give us into the prophetic office of Christ?

> a. Acts 3:22–23
> b. Luke 13:33
> c. John 8:26–28

3. The classic text describing the function of a priest is Hebrews 5:1. What does this text tell us about priests?

4. The priestly work of Christ involves what two tasks according to the following scriptures?

> a. Hebrews 10:14
> b. Hebrews 7:25

5. What do the following texts teach us about the kingship of Christ?

> a. Psalm 2:6
> b. Isaiah 9:6–7

c. Daniel 7:14

d. Luke 1:33

e. Acts 2:30–36

f. Colossians 1:13

g. Revelation 1:5

DISCUSSION GUIDE

1. How would you describe the relationship between the Word of God incarnate, the Word of God written, and the Word of God preached?

2. According to Hebrews, Jesus fulfilled everything the Old Testament sacrifices and priesthood symbolized when, as the great High Priest, He offered Himself once and for all. If you discussed the Roman Catholic priesthood and the sacrifice of the Mass with a Roman Catholic, how would the book of Hebrews inform your discussion?

3. When Scripture speaks of Jesus as the "ruler over the kings of the earth" (Rev. 1:5), does that mean that every national government should explicitly and publicly express its submission to Jesus Christ prior to the second coming of Christ? Why or why not?

APPLICATION

1. Jesus intercedes always for us, and we are called to intercede in prayer for others. Take time right now to pray for someone you know who is suffering.

2. Take time this week to meditate on each of Christ's offices. Consider how each serves toward your salvation.

SUGGESTED READING FOR FURTHER STUDY

Bavinck, Herman. *Reformed Dogmatics,* vol. 3, pp. 364–8.

Berkhof, Louis. *Systematic Theology,* pp. 356–66, 406–12.

Calvin, John. *Institutes of the Christian Religion,* 2.15.

Hodge, Charles. *Systematic Theology,* vol. 2, pp. 459–79, 596–609.

Owen, John. *The Works of John Owen,* vol. 1, pp. 85–100.

8

LAST SUPPER

THE POPULAR ENTHUSIASM THAT accompanied Jesus' triumphal entry to Jerusalem was tempered by the opposition of the Jewish religious leaders. In the week that followed, they questioned Him and tested Him at every step. Thus, the storm clouds began to gather, and the situation quickly became ominous.

Luke wrote:

> Now the Feast of Unleavened Bread drew near, which is called Passover. And the chief priests and the scribes sought how they might kill Him, for they feared the people. Then Satan entered Judas, surnamed Iscariot, who was numbered among the twelve. So he went his way and conferred with the chief priests and captains,

how he might betray Him to them. And they were glad, and agreed to give him money. So he promised and sought opportunity to betray Him to them in the absence of the multitude. (22:1–6)

So deep was the opposition of the leaders to Jesus that they entered into a conspiracy to do away with Him. That conspiracy received a major boost when Judas Iscariot, prompted by Satan, went to them and offered to betray Jesus to them.

While this was happening, Jesus was preparing to celebrate the Passover with His disciples: "Then came the Day of Unleavened Bread, when the Passover must be killed. And He sent Peter and John, saying, 'Go and prepare the Passover for us, that we may eat.'... When the hour had come, He sat down, and the twelve apostles with Him. Then He said to them, 'With fervent desire I have desired to eat this Passover with you before I suffer; for I say to you, I will no longer eat of it until it is fulfilled in the kingdom of God'" (vv. 7–8, 14–16).

At this point, Jesus was beginning to enter His passion, His final suffering and death. Luke made this clear when he wrote, "When the hour had come" (22:14). Throughout His ministry, Jesus made a number of references to His "hour," and John's gospel uses the term several times (John 2:4; 7:30; 8:20; 17:1). For instance, he wrote, "Now before the Feast of the Passover, when Jesus knew that His hour had come that He should depart from this world to the Father, having loved His own who were in the world, He loved them to the end" (13:1). The "hour" in Jesus' life had to do with the culmination of His mission.

While Jesus knew that glorification would follow His passion, His immediate future was dark and ghastly. The hour of crisis was at hand, and He realized that His hours of life in His body were numbered. It was less than twenty-four hours before He would die; apart from His postresurrection life, this was to be His last night alive in the body on earth. Because of this, He had a great desire to celebrate the Passover with His disciples one last time, so He made provision for them to gather in the upper room to keep the feast.

The Passover celebration was very important to the Jewish people. God had commanded them to observe it every year without fail to commemorate His redemptive action in delivering His people from slavery in Egypt. God commanded Pharaoh to let the people go, but Pharaoh refused (Exod. 5:1–2). God then sent ten horrendous plagues on the Egyptians—the waters became blood; frogs, lice, flies, and locusts infested the land; hail destroyed the crops; and so on (Exod. 7–10). The last and the worst of the plagues was the death of all the firstborn in the land, both sons and livestock. God brought death on the Egyptians and the house of Pharaoh. However, He took intricate steps to spare the lives of the Israelites' firstborn children and livestock. Each family was commanded to select a lamb without blemish, kill it, and smear the blood of the lamb on the doorposts of the home to identify it as the abode of a family of God's people. He then promised that He would "pass over" those houses (Exod. 12).

As a result of that plague, the greatest redemptive act in the Old Testament took place—God spared His people, then delivered them out of the hands of Pharaoh and out of bondage in Egypt.

Thus, the Passover was celebrated every year in Israel, and every father was required to explain to his children the meaning behind the feast (Exod. 12:25–27).

So, the first purpose of the Passover was to celebrate something that had taken place in the past, the deliverance from Egypt. However, not only did this celebration direct the Israelites' thoughts backward in time, but it pointed forward to the final Passover, when the perfect Lamb would be sacrificed, ending the sacrificial system once and for all. It was understood that by the blood of that Lamb, the people would experience not merely an exodus out of the bondage of Pharaoh, but an exodus from the bondage of death itself, an exodus that would take them into the Promised Land of heaven.

OLD RITE, NEW MEANING

So, Jesus gathered His disciples in the upper room for the Passover meal. But as He was going through the liturgy of the Passover, He changed it. This was audacious, but Jesus was the one person in the world who had the authority to do it. After all, the Passover was about Him because He is the Lamb of God. He had the right to give a new meaning to this Old Testament rite. He was about to fulfill the Passover, so it was entirely appropriate and timely for Him to make the changes He instituted that night.

Of course, what happened in the upper room that night was not simply the fulfillment of the Passover; it was the end of the old covenant. In that night, the New Testament church was born.

Most people believe the church was born on the day of Pentecost. I disagree. I think the church was born when Jesus instituted the new covenant. When covenants were instituted, they had to be ratified by blood, and the ratification of the new covenant Jesus instituted in the upper room took place the following afternoon when He spilled His own blood. This was a cardinal moment in redemptive history, the end of the old covenant and the beginning of the new covenant.

Luke wrote, "And He took bread, gave thanks and broke it, and gave it to them, saying, 'This is My body which is given for you; do this in remembrance of Me'" (22:19). There has been endless controversy about what Jesus meant when He said, "This is My body." Was He identifying Himself with the bread? Did He use the word *is* as a copula, showing that bread is identical to His body? Many have thought so and many think so today. In the debates among the Reformers over the meaning of the Lord's Supper, Martin Luther insisted that the bread is literally the body of Christ. He pounded on the table and shouted, "*Hoc est corpus meum. Hoc est corpus meum,*" the Latin for "This is My body."

However, Jesus also made numerous statements such as "I am the door" (John 10:9), but no one thinks that Jesus must be literally identified with oak, veneer, doorknobs, and hinges. We understand that the word *is* can mean "represents." This seems especially likely in the case of the bread, since Jesus took an element that had symbolized something in the past. He simply gave it a new symbolism, telling His disciples that thenceforth it would represent His body, His life, given for the remission of their sins.

Luke went on to say, "Likewise He also took the cup after supper, saying, 'This cup is the new covenant in My blood, which is shed for you'" (22:20). During the Passover celebration, participants drank from the cup four different times. So, Jesus again changed the liturgy and said that the cup would represent His blood—another picture of His life and a reminder of His sacrificial death. As Paul explained, "As often as you eat this bread and drink this cup, you proclaim the Lord's death till He comes" (1 Cor. 11:26).

It is interesting to me that in the early church, the Christians celebrated this new covenant sacrament not just once a year but once a week, because they understood it to be vitally important in communicating the significance of the cross, the new covenant, and the Lamb who was slain. That is what we celebrate every time we come together in the church and enjoy the Lord's Supper.

THE MEANING OF THE SUPPER

Sadly, churches are hopelessly divided in their understanding of what happens in the celebration of the Lord's Supper. Not only are the debates lengthy, but they become quite acerbic at times. Everyone understands that this is an extremely important rite, so passions can become inflamed. How are we to cut through the confusion and understand the Lord's Supper accurately?

The Roman Catholic Church developed the doctrine of transubstantiation, which teaches that in the miracle of the Mass, the bread and the wine are changed into the substance of the body and blood of Christ. This means that Jesus is corporeally, physically there in the bread and wine. This doctrine is based on the teaching of Aristotle, who said every object has both substance and "accidents," which are external, perceivable qualities. Rome said the substance of the bread and wine changes into the substance of the body and blood of Christ, but the accidents of bread and wine remain the same, which means that the bread still looks like bread, tastes like bread, smells like bread, feels like bread, and so on. The same is true for the wine. They still have the outward qualities of bread and wine, but they are no longer bread and wine. In their substance, their essence, they are the body and blood of Christ.

Luther thought the doctrine of transubstantiation involved more miracles than were necessary. He said there is no change of substance, but that Christ is present in, under, and through the elements. Still, like transubstantiation, his doctrine (known as consubstantiation) insists on the real, physical presence of Christ in the Lord's Supper.

John Calvin had a problem with that idea. He remembered the Council of Chalcedon in AD 451, when the church declared that in the mystery of the incarnation, Christ had two natures. The divine nature and the human nature were joined together in perfect unity, and that union was without mixture, confusion, separation, or division, each nature retaining its own attributes. The human nature of Jesus was not deified but retained its human attributes, and the divine nature was not humanized but retained its divine attributes. So, the divine nature can be in many places at once, but not the human nature, which is limited in space and time by the "creatureliness" of the body.

Both the Roman Catholic Church and Luther responded with the doctrine of the communication of attributes, which teaches that Jesus' human body was able to be in many places at the same time because the divine nature communicates the power of ubiquity or omnipresence to the human nature. I am convinced that teaching is a serious violation of Chalcedon and represents a docetic view of Jesus, a view that completely destroys the reality of His human nature.

I believe that when the church receives the Lord's Supper, Jesus is truly present, but He is present by His divine nature. His divine nature is not separated from the human nature. The human nature and the divine nature are both in heaven, but the divine nature is also here. We are connected to the whole Jesus by virtue of the presence of the divine nature.

Still other believers go in the opposite direction and argue that the Lord's Supper is merely symbolic. They say the elements of the sacrament represent Jesus, but there is no divine or human presence of Christ in the sacrament.

These debates will go on and on, precisely because the church understands that when Jesus celebrated the Passover for the last time on the night before He died, He intended to establish a sacrament that would cause His people to remember what He accomplished by offering the perfect sacrifice, but also cause them to look forward to the ultimate banquet feast in heaven at the marriage feast of the Lamb.

CHAPTER 8

STUDY GUIDE

INTRODUCTION

In the Old Testament, the Passover lamb distinguished the people of God from the unbelieving Egyptians. The Passover also marked Israel's redemption from Egypt. The Old Testament prophets described the future redemption of Israel in terms of a new exodus. In this chapter, Dr. R. C. Sproul looks at the Last Supper, showing how Christ is our Passover Lamb in this meal that marks the arrival of the greater exodus, redemption from slavery to sin and death.

LEARNING OBJECTIVES

1. To be able to explain the significance of the Old Testament Passover.
2. To be able to explain the basic meaning of the Lord's Supper.

QUOTATIONS

> The cup of blessing which we bless, is it not the communion of the blood of Christ? The bread which we break, is it not the communion of the body of Christ?
>
> —1 Corinthians 10:16

> If Christ is our head, and dwells in us, he communicates to us his life; and we have nothing to hope from until we are united to his body. The whole reality of the sacred Supper consists in this—Christ, by grafting us into his body, not only makes us partakers of his body and blood, but infuses into us the life whose fullness resides in himself: for his flesh is not eaten for any other end than to give us life.
>
> —John Calvin, *Tracts Relating to the Reformation*

OUTLINE

I. Introduction

A. Jesus was received enthusiastically by the multitudes, but the religious establishment was outraged by His triumphal entry.

B. In Luke 22, we are told that just as the Feast of Unleavened Bread was being prepared, the religious leaders were entering into a conspiracy to do away with Jesus.

C. At the same time, Jesus was preparing to celebrate the Passover with His disciples.

II. When the Hour Had Come

A. At this point, Jesus was entering into what is called His "passion."

B. Jesus was fully aware of His impending execution.

C. As they are preparing for the Passover, we read, "When the hour had come" (Luke 22:14).

D. Throughout His ministry, multiple references are made to Jesus' "hour."

E. Many times, He said, "My hour has not yet come."

F. The hour of crisis was now at hand.

III. The Passover

    A. The Passover commemorated God's redemptive action in saving His people at the time of the exodus.

    B. During the tenth plague, God instructed His people to place the blood of a lamb on their doors.

    C. God would pass over the houses of those marked with the blood of the lamb and spare their firstborn.

    D. After sparing the Israelites and judging the Egyptians, God brought His people out of slavery in Egypt.

    E. The Passover was celebrated every year, and the father was required to explain the meaning of the meal to the children.

    F. The Passover was a call to remembrance, a celebration of something that had taken place in the past.

    G. The Passover also looked forward to the future when the perfect Passover Lamb would be sacrificed, ending the sacrificial system once and for all.

    H. The future Passover would mark the beginning of a new and greater exodus out of the bondage of sin.

IV. The Last Supper

    A. After gathering His disciples for the Passover, Jesus began going through the Passover liturgy, and He changed it.

    B. The only person in the world with the authority to change the Passover liturgy was Jesus because the Passover was about Him.

C. Jesus was the Passover Lamb.

D. In the upper room, the New Testament church was born.

E. The new covenant established in the upper room was ratified the next day in Jesus' own blood.

F. After He took the bread, He changed the meaning of the bread by saying, "This is My body."

G. There is great controversy about what Jesus meant when He spoke these words.

H. Jesus also changed the meaning of the cup, saying, "This cup is the new covenant in My blood, which is shed for you" (Luke 22:20).

I. It is interesting to note that in the early church, Christians celebrated this new covenant sacrament once a week because it was understood to be so important.

V. The Meaning of the Supper

A. Churches are divided in their understanding of what happens in the celebration of the Lord's Supper.

B. The Roman Catholic Church developed the doctrine of transubstantiation, arguing that the substance of the bread and wine change while the "accidents" remain the same.

C. Martin Luther argued that there is no change in the substance of the bread, but that Christ is in, under, and with the elements.

D. John Calvin disagreed with both views because of the doctrine of Christ taught at the Council of Chalcedon.

E. According to Chalcedon, the human nature of Christ is not deified; it retains its own attributes.

F. The human nature is limited in space.

G. Rome and Luther got around that with their doctrine of the communication of attributes.

H. Dr. Sproul's church believes that Christ is present by His divine nature.

BIBLE STUDY

1. Read Exodus 12:1–51 and answer the following questions:

    a. Why is it significant that God told Moses that this Passover would be the beginning of a new calendar for Israel?

    b. What principal thing did God command the Israelites to do in preparation for the Passover?

    c. Did the Passover distinguish between the act of sacrifice and the sacrificial meal? If so, is the eating of the lamb the act of sacrifice or the sacrificial meal? Is such a distinction significant? Why or why not?

    d. What prerequisite for participation in the Passover is emphasized repeatedly in Exodus 12:43–48?

2. Read Matthew 26:26. What four things did Jesus do with the bread? What two things did He tell the disciples to do with the bread? What did Jesus say about the bread? Normally, the Passover liturgy would include the following words: "This is the bread of affliction which our ancestors ate when they came from the land of Egypt." Is it reasonable to suppose that the Jews who used these words believed they were eating the very pieces of bread that their ancestors had eaten and digested? Is it more reasonable to suppose that the Jews used this language to point to their own real participation in the act of redemption that their ancestors had experienced firsthand? How does our understanding of the words used in the normal Passover liturgy help our understanding of Jesus' words about the bread?

DISCUSSION GUIDE

1. The Passover was a communal, family-oriented sacrament of the old covenant. What significance, if any, does this have for our understanding of the Lord's Supper?

2. The Roman Catholic Church defines a sacrament as "a symbol of a sacred thing." Does the doctrine of transubstantiation conflict with this definition? If so, how?

3. How do the Roman Catholic and Lutheran doctrines of the Lord's Supper conflict with the definition of Chalcedon?

APPLICATION

1. Reflect on what it means to be saved from the wrath of God, to have God's judgment pass over you. The next time you partake of the Lord's Supper, give thanks (Eucharist) to God for marking you with the blood of the Lamb and sparing you from His judgment and wrath.

2. Reflect on what you have learned in this chapter that will help you as you approach the Lord's Table in the future.

SUGGESTED READING FOR FURTHER STUDY

Armstrong, John H., ed. *Understanding Four Views on the Lord's Supper.*

Torrance, Thomas F., ed. *The Mystery of the Lord's Supper: Sermons by Robert Bruce.*

Calvin, John. "Short Treatise on the Supper of Our Lord" in *Tracts and Letters,* vol. 2, pp. 163–98.

Calvin, John. *Institutes of the Christian Religion,* 4.17.

Davies, W. D., and D. C. Allison. *Matthew 19–28,* pp. 464–78.

France, R. T. *The Gospel of Matthew,* pp. 980–96.

Mathison, Keith A. *Given for You.*

Motyer, J. A. *The Message of Exodus,* pp. 126–55.

Stuart, Douglas K. *Exodus,* pp. 269–311.

9

CRUCIFIXION

THE APOSTLE PAUL MADE the famous statement that he was "determined not to know anything among you except Jesus Christ and Him crucified" (1 Cor. 2:2). Of course, we know that was an example of Apostolic hyperbole, because Paul knew considerably more and wrote on many other subjects besides the cross of Christ. Paul was simply declaring the singular importance of the crucifixion of Christ, which was the zenith of His work, the high point of the mission He was sent to accomplish.

If we had been eyewitnesses of the crucifixion, I doubt we would have realized that we were observing an act of cosmic significance. The people who were gathered there at Golgotha had many different perspectives on what they were seeing. From the viewpoint of Caiaphas, the high priest, the execution of Jesus was a political expediency to keep the Romans off the back of the Jewish Sanhedrin. For Pontius Pilate, the Roman governor, it was also an act of political expediency in order to calm the tumultuous crowd that was screaming for the blood of Christ. For the thief on the cross, who recognized the identity of Jesus, it was a miscarriage of justice. But which of the observers realized that Jesus was making atonement for sin?

To understand the depth of what happened at the cross, we have to look to the epistles of the New Testament, wherein the meaning of the event is interpreted for us. Paul wrote:

> But now the righteousness of God apart from the law is revealed, being witnessed by the Law and the Prophets, even the righteousness of God, through faith in Jesus Christ, to all and on all who believe. For there is no difference; for all have sinned and fall short of the glory of God, being justified freely by His grace through the redemption that is in Christ Jesus, whom God set forth as a propitiation by His blood, through faith, to demonstrate His righteousness, because in His forbearance God had passed over the sins that were previously committed, to demonstrate at the present time His righteousness, that He might be just and the justifier of the one who has faith in Jesus. (Rom. 3:21–26)

The Apostle made two comments here in reference to our justification as it relates to the work of Jesus. The first of these is his reference to the act of propitiation in Jesus' death. What did Paul mean?

A Jew reading this material would understand it in light of the annual celebration of the Day of Atonement, Yom Kippur. This was one of the high points of the year in the life of Israel. On that day, the high priest had to make an offering of a bull as a sacrifice for himself, eventually sprinkling some of the bull's blood on the mercy seat in the Holy of Holies (Lev. 16:11–14). Then the high priest was to kill a goat as a sin offering for the people and sprinkle some of the goat's blood on the mercy seat (v. 15). Next he was to take a live goat, lay his hands on its head, and confess the sins of the people of Israel, symbolically transferring their sins to the goat, which was then led away into the wilderness, taking the sins of the people with it (vv. 20–22).

The mercy seat was regarded as the throne of God. It was the golden lid on the ark of the covenant, which was crowned by two golden cherubim (Exod. 25:17–22). So, in this ritual, blood was sprinkled on the throne of God, indicating a sacrifice to satisfy the demands of God's justice. The Hebrew word that is translated as "mercy seat" is best translated as "propitiatory." Thus, an act of propitiation is an act of satisfaction.

This concept and the need for it is somewhat foreign to us because we have been told so often that God is a God of love, a God of mercy, a God of grace who forgives our sins freely. We think that all God has to do to reconcile us to Himself is to simply dispense His forgiveness to us. But when we think like this, we forget that God is holy and just. This is why Paul wrote in Romans 3 that God "set [Jesus] forth as a propitiation by His blood, through faith, to demonstrate His righteousness … that He might be just and the justifier of the one who has faith in Jesus" (vv. 25–26). When God justifies His people, He does not do it by a unilateral act of forgiveness, because to do so without propitiation, without satisfaction, without atonement would be a complete violation of His justice. God will not wink at sin. He simply will not pass over it without exacting a punishment for it. The elaborate ritual of the Day of Atonement shows us the need for a blood sacrifice to propitiate the wrath of God and satisfy His justice.

The book of Hebrews reminds us that the blood of bulls and goats cannot atone for our sins (10:4). The elaborate business of killing animals and sprinkling their blood on the mercy seat never saved anyone, because there was no inherent, intrinsic value in the blood of the bulls and goats to effect propitiation. So, how were the sins of the people forgiven in the Old Testament? It was not on the basis of the blood of the animals, but on the basis of the blood of Christ, who was yet to come. All of the observations and rituals in the tabernacle and later in the temple pointed beyond themselves to the future reality that would satisfy the demands of God's righteousness and justice.

THE WORK OF REDEMPTION

Paul also wrote that we are "justified freely by His grace through the redemption that is in Christ Jesus" (Rom. 3:24). The concept of redemption is also linked to the work of Jesus at the cross. Redemption is an act of purchasing, an economic act. At the cross, Jesus purchased His people by redeeming them or paying the price of their redemption.

The Old Testament prophet Hosea was given the difficult task of acting out God's love for His wayward people by marrying a harlot, Gomer (Hosea 1:2–3). Later, Gomer apparently left Hosea and fell into an adulterous relationship and some sort of slavery or servitude. Therefore, Hosea bought her for himself (3:1–3). By purchasing her, Hosea redeemed her. Thus, we can see how the concept of redemption became associated with the idea of salvation.

The New Testament teaches that Jesus purchased His people out of bondage to the world, the flesh, and the Devil (Gal. 4:3; 5:1). That's why Paul said, "You were bought at a price" (1 Cor. 6:20; 7:23). Believers have been purchased, and the price was the blood of Christ, the life of Christ, for in Jewish categories the life was in the blood. In the Old Testament, it was not enough to scratch an animal to get blood for a sacrifice. The animal had to shed its blood in death, and so did Christ to pay for sins.

Again, in the Old Testament picture of redemption, many times the one who would make the purchase to buy someone out of slavery was a relative (Lev. 25:47–49). That relative was known as the kinsman-redeemer, the person who would pay for the liberation of his brother, sister, mother, or other relative. In the book of Ruth, Boaz functions as a kinsman-redeemer for Ruth. Likewise, in New Testament categories, Jesus is the supreme

Kinsman-Redeemer, who makes payment for His adopted children on the cross.

BLESSING AND CURSE

Paul made an astonishing statement in his letter to the Galatians:

> For as many as are of the works of the law are under the curse; for it is written, "Cursed is everyone who does not continue in all the things which are written in the book of the law, to do them." But that no one is justified by the law in the sight of God is evident, for "the just shall live by faith." Yet the law is not of faith, but "the man who does them shall live by them." Christ has redeemed us from the curse of the law, having become a curse for us (for it is written, "Cursed is everyone who hangs on a tree"), that the blessing of Abraham might come upon the Gentiles in Christ Jesus, that we might receive the promise of the Spirit through faith. (3:10–14)

Paul reached back into the terms of the Old Testament covenant that God made with Moses. When the covenant was renewed, as recounted in the book of Deuteronomy, Moses said to the people, as he gathered them together in solemn assembly:

"Now it shall come to pass, if you diligently obey the voice of the LORD your God, to observe carefully all His commandments which I command you today, that the LORD your God will set you high above all nations of the earth. And all these blessings shall come upon you and overtake you, because you obey the voice of the LORD your God" (28:1–2). He then proceeded to list a multitude of ways in which the Israelites would be blessed, a comprehensive catalog of prosperity.

However, Moses went on to say, "But it shall come to pass, if you do not obey the voice of the LORD your God, to observe carefully all His commandments and His statutes which I command you today, that all these curses will come upon you and overtake you" (v. 15). He then set forth a far longer list of curses that would come down upon the Israelites if they disobeyed.

We understand, of course, that the world and the human race were already under a curse because of the sin of our first parents, Adam and Eve. God pronounced curses on the Serpent, then on the man and his wife (Gen. 3). But what was that curse?

I like to explain it in terms of the Hebrew benediction that Aaron was commanded to pronounce on the Israelites: "The LORD bless you and keep you; the LORD make His face shine upon you, and be gracious to you; the LORD lift up His countenance upon you, and give you peace" (Num. 6:24–26). This is an example of Hebrew poetry using synonymous parallelism, where each line means the same thing. For the Jew, "The LORD bless you" meant the same thing as "The LORD make His face shine upon you" and "The LORD lift up His countenance upon you." The Jews understood that the supreme blessing would be to see God face-to-face someday. This, then, was the blessing, but the curse was the polar opposite. To be cursed of God was to have Him curse you, turn His face away from you, and abandon you.

With that background, we can understand what Paul was getting at when he said, "Christ has redeemed us from the curse of the law, having become a curse for us (for it is written, 'Cursed is everyone who hangs on a tree'), that the blessing of Abraham might come upon the Gentiles in Christ Jesus, that we might receive the promise of the Spirit through faith" (Gal. 3:13–14). In order for people to be able to receive the blessing that was promised to Abraham and to his seed, sin had to be punished. Jesus not only took the curse on Himself, but also became the curse. He was completely forsaken by the Father. He cried out from the cross, "My God, My God, why have You forsaken Me?" (Mark 15:34) when the Father turned His back. Once all of our sins were imputed to Jesus, He was the most loathsome sight ever in the universe, and God is too holy to even look at sin. So, He turned His back on Jesus, that Jesus might be cursed, but that we might not be cursed, and instead be blessed.

When people discuss the crucifixion, they often go on and on about the physical pain Jesus endured because of the thorns, the nails, and the spear that pierced His side. I wonder whether Jesus even felt those things. There were thousands of people who died like that, but only one received the fullness of the curse of God in the middle of His crucifixion. That pain was far worse than anything His body endured.

Finally, before Jesus yielded up His spirit, He said, "It is finished!" (John 19:30). He then committed Himself into the hands of the One who had just cursed Him and was received once more into the Father's presence. The humiliation, the suffering, the curse were finished.

One of my favorite Christmas carols is "Joy to the World," which includes a line that says, "He comes to make His blessings flow far as the curse is found." The hymn writer here is referring to the efficacy of Christ's work of redemption. It reached as far as the curse was found.

CHAPTER 9

STUDY GUIDE

INTRODUCTION

The apex of Christ's redemptive work occurred when He was nailed to the cross and bore the penalty due to us. His crucifixion was an act of propitiation, satisfying the justice of God. In this chapter, Dr. R. C. Sproul explains what happened on the cross, how Christ was both a propitiation for sin and our Redeemer.

LEARNING OBJECTIVES

1. To be able to explain how Christ was our propitiation on the cross.
2. To be able to explain what it means for Christ to be our Redeemer.

QUOTATIONS

> When I survey the wondrous cross
> On which the Prince of glory died,
> My richest gain I count but loss,
> And pour contempt on all my pride.
>
> —Isaac Watts, "When I Survey
> the Wondrous Cross"

> In pagan propitiation, *a human being* offers a propitiatory sacrifice to make a god propitious. In Christian propitiation, *God the Father* sets forth Jesus as the propitiation to make *himself* propitious; God is both the subject and the object of propitiation. God is the one who provides the sacrifice precisely as a way of turning aside his own wrath. God the Father is thus the propitia*tor* and the propitia*ted,* and God the Son is the propitia*tion.*
>
> —D. A. Carson, *Scandalous: The Cross and Resurrection of Jesus*

OUTLINE

I. Introduction

A. The Apostle Paul said that he was determined to know nothing except Christ and Him crucified.

B. What Paul was saying was that in the crucifixion we reach the zenith of the work of Christ.

C. It is unlikely that eyewitnesses of the crucifixion realized that they were witnessing an act of atonement.

D. We see the interpretation of the crucifixion in the New Testament epistles.

II. Propitiation

A. In Romans 3:21–26, Paul made two comments in reference to our justification as it relates to the work of Jesus.

B. Paul said that in the shedding of Christ's blood, there occurred an act of propitiation.

C. The Jew who read this would understand it in light of the Day of Atonement.

D. On the Day of Atonement, the high priest would enter the Holy of Holies and sprinkle blood on the mercy seat—the throne of God.

E. This act symbolized that a sacrifice of blood was necessary in order to satisfy the demands of God's justice.

F. Propitiation is an act of satisfaction.

G. God does not justify people by a unilateral act of forgiveness because to do so without propitiation would be a violation of His justice.

H. Hebrews reminds us that the blood of bulls and goats cannot atone for sin.

I. Old Testament believers were forgiven on the basis of the blood of Christ, who was yet to come.

III. Redemption

A. Christ was also sent to bring redemption.

B. Redemption is an act of purchasing.

C. In the Old Testament, some people would place themselves in indentured servitude to pay off a debt.

D. We were redeemed out of servitude by the blood of Christ.

E. Jesus is the supreme Kinsman-Redeemer, and the payment price is the blood He shed on the cross.

III. The Curse Bearer

A. In Galatians 3, Paul wrote that Christ has redeemed us from the curse of the law.

B. The curse is the opposite of blessing.

C. In order for the blessing promised to Abraham to be received, sin had to be punished.

D. Jesus not only took the curse upon Himself, but also became the curse.

E. Once Jesus had all of our sins imputed to Him, He was the most loathsome sight ever in the universe.

F. God placed the curse on Jesus in order that we might not bear the curse ourselves.

G. Jesus bore the curse for a season, but the story didn't end on Friday.

BIBLE STUDY

1. Read Isaiah 52:13–53:12 and Psalm 22, and then read the crucifixion account in Matthew 27:24–56. How do these Old Testament texts inform our understanding of what occurred on the cross?

2. Read the following Old Testament texts, noting their context. How did the crucifixion fulfill these Old Testament prophecies, and given their context, what is the significance for our understanding of the crucifixion?

    a. Psalm 69:21

    b. Ezekiel 37

    c. Amos 8:9

    d. Zechariah 14:4–5

3. Compare the taunting of Jesus in Matthew 27:40 to the tempta-tion narrative in Matthew 4:3 and 6. Does this give us any clues about what is going on at the crucifixion?

DISCUSSION GUIDE

1. Dr. Sproul wrote that once Jesus had all of our sins imputed to Him, He was the most loathsome sight ever in the universe. Many churches throughout history have artistically portrayed the crucifixion in almost serene tones. Regardless of your convictions concerning the appropriateness of artistic representations of the crucifixion, do you think that Christ's bearing of sin, His becom-ing the curse on our behalf, and His suffering the wrath of God on the cross were purely on a spiritual level, or did He become the most loathsome sight ever in the universe?

2. The theologian Henri Blocher has written concerning the cru-cifixion that God here "makes the supreme crime, the murder of the only righteous person, the very operation that abolishes sin."[1] How does this tie in to Israel's entire history of almost uninter-rupted rebellion? How does Genesis 50:20 shed light on this great mystery?

APPLICATION

1. Read and meditate on Colossians 1:13–14 today. Reflect on what it means for you that Christ accomplished all of this for you through suffering the penalty for your sin on the cross.

2. Paul decided to know nothing except Jesus Christ and Him crucified (1 Cor. 2:2). This entire study is about Jesus Christ and Him crucified, the person and work of Christ. Thank God for His amazing grace shown toward you in Christ.

SUGGESTED READING FOR FURTHER STUDY

Carson, D. A. *Scandalous: The Cross and Resurrection of Jesus.*

France, R. T. *The Gospel of Matthew,* pp. 1059–85.

Hodge, A. A. *The Atonement.*

Lane, William L. *The Gospel according to Mark,* pp. 558–77.

Owen, John. *The Death of Death in the Death of Christ.*

Ridderbos, Herman. *The Gospel of John,* pp. 607–24.

Ryken, Philip G. *The Message of Salvation,* pp. 90–117.

Sproul, R. C. *The Truth of the Cross.*

NOTES: CHAPTER 9

1. Henri Blocher, *Evil and the Cross: An Analytical Look at the Problem of Pain* (Grand Rapids, MI: Kregel, 1994), 132.

10

RESURRECTION

WHEN JESUS CRIED OUT "It is finished" and yielded His spirit up to the Father, He was truly dead. His spirit left His body and went to be with the Father, so the body He left behind was a corpse. Like any other corpse, there was no heartbeat, there were no brain waves, there was no blood pulsating through His veins. Jesus was dead, and as a dead man in His humanity, He was utterly powerless to do any significant work.

It may seem a bit strange, then, to include the resurrection of Christ in a study of His work. Given that He was powerless, He was completely passive in His resurrection. He did not raise Himself from the dead, but rather He was raised by the power of the Holy Spirit. Nevertheless, the resurrection was a vitally important part of the work He accomplished.

To understand how this can be so, let me direct your attention to the words of Paul in his first epistle to the Corinthians:

> But now Christ is risen from the dead, and has become the firstfruits of those who have fallen asleep. For since by man came death, by Man also came the resurrection of the dead. For as in Adam all die, even so in Christ all shall be made alive. But each one in his own order: Christ the firstfruits, afterward those who are Christ's at His coming. Then comes the end, when He delivers the kingdom to God the Father, when He puts an end to all rule and all authority and power. For He must reign till He has put all enemies under His feet. The last enemy that will be destroyed is death. For "He has put all things under His feet." (15:20–27a)

In this Apostolic interpretation of the significance of the resurrection, we see once again the biblical comparison of our original progenitor as the first Adam and Jesus as the new Adam, a theme we examined earlier. The first Adam brought death into the world. The new Adam, Christ, brought resurrection from the dead.

So, in the resurrection, Christ triumphed over the supreme enemy that afflicts human life, death. Here we see *Christus Victor,* Christ the Victor, who triumphed not only over Satan and sin but also over death itself. But that victory was not simply for Himself. The Apostle said here that He became the firstfruits, so that in the resurrection God did not only raise Jesus from the dead, but also raised all who are in Christ, so that we participate in that triumph over death. This is why the resurrection of Christ is so important to the Christian faith. It is the reason why we join together for worship every Sunday instead of Saturday, for it was on Sunday that Christ was raised from the dead. We call that the Lord's Day, and it has become the new Sabbath.

RAISED BY THE COMMAND OF GOD

We see a parallel to Jesus' passivity and powerlessness in the person of Lazarus, as he lay in his tomb after his death. When Lazarus was raised from the dead, he contributed nothing to it. Lazarus had been dead for four days, and when Christ came and raised him from the dead, He did not go into the tomb and give Lazarus mouth-to-mouth resuscitation. Neither did He plead with Lazarus's corpse, saying, "Come now, Lazarus; get yourself together." Rather, He called with a loud voice, "Lazarus, come forth!" (John 11:43). At the command of the Son of God, the dead body of Lazarus came back to life.

I cite this parallel to highlight the way in which Lazarus was raised. It was very similar to creation. How was the universe brought into being? Did life come to pass through the chance collision of atoms in the primordial slime? No. It all happened by divine imperative, by the command of the eternal, omnipotent God. He said, "Let there be light," and there was light (Gen. 1:3).

The sheer power of the divine command brought life into reality in the first place, and it brought Lazarus back from the dead.

The Holy Spirit was there at creation, hovering over the waters (Gen. 1:2), and that same Spirit went into the tomb where the corpse of Jesus lay and brought life out of death. Early that Sunday morning, suddenly Jesus' eyelids fluttered, brain activity began, the heart started to beat, and the blood started to course through His veins. By the power of the Holy Spirit, He came out of the grave clothes, out of the state of death, and returned to life, victorious over the grave.

Many people believe the resurrection is the ultimate unbelievable miracle. Skeptics say that if there is anything we know for sure, it is that when people die, they stay dead. So, among those tenets of Christianity that are popularly regarded as mythological, the resurrection usually tops the list. However, the New Testament looks at it from a completely different perspective. In his sermon on the day of Pentecost, Peter said, "God raised [Him] up, having loosed the pains of death, because it was not possible that He should be held by it" (Acts 2:24). Death had no claim over Jesus. Death is the punishment God gives to beings for sin, but Jesus was sinless. Of course when He took our sin by imputation on the cross, He was filled with sin, but not His own. His inherent sinlessness denied death the authority to contain Him. So it was not just *possible* for Jesus to rise again; it was *impossible* that He would *not* be raised from the dead. How can death hold a sinless human being? It cannot. So Jesus was vindicated in the resurrection.

The New Testament tells us that Jesus "was delivered up because of our offenses, and was raised because of our justification"

(Rom. 4:25). He lived and He died for our justification, but He also was raised for our justification. The whole process by which we are made right with God in justification rests on the work of Jesus through His life, His death, and His resurrection.

But how does the resurrection bear on our justification? If Jesus had lived a life of perfect obedience and offered Himself as a perfect sacrifice once and for all in His death, how would we know the sacrifice satisfied God? How would we know that His offering actually propitiated the Father? In the resurrection, the Father said that He received the perfect sacrifice of Christ. He accepted it for the justification of the ungodly. Therefore, the Father said, "I am satisfied," and removed the curse from us.

RAISED TO INCORRUPTION

The Apostle Paul wrote, "The body is sown in corruption, it is raised in incorruption. It is sown in dishonor, it is raised in glory. It is sown in weakness, it is raised in power" (1 Cor. 15:42b–43). Paul was speaking here of the decay that comes on corpses. This was made most vivid in the story of Lazarus. When Jesus commanded that the stone be rolled away from the entrance of Lazarus's tomb, Lazarus's sister Martha said, "Lord, by this time there is a stench, for he has been dead four days" (John 11:39b). The King James Version renders Martha's words this way: "He stinketh." The stench that goes with the corruption of the flesh was part of the reality of the death and the burial of Lazarus, just as it accompanies every death.

But Paul spoke not only of corruption but also of incorruption. When Jesus was raised from the dead, it was not merely a resuscitation. His body was not just as it had been before He died. Of course, there was continuity between the body that went into the tomb and the body that came out. It looked the same. It was still identifiable by the marks of the nails, the spear, and such. Jesus could be recognized. But there was also a dramatic change in the body. When He rose again, His body was not simply restored, it was also glorified. The pattern of humiliation that persisted throughout Jesus' life was dramatically reversed when He came forth from the tomb. His resurrection was the first step in a dramatic exaltation.

When Paul said the body is raised in incorruption, he meant that the body that came out of Jesus' tomb could never suffer decay or corruption in the flesh. Likewise, when our bodies are raised to new life, they will never again deteriorate. They will never again be subject to the ravages of time and disease. They will be incorruptible. They will be glorified.

Paul also said the body "is sown in dishonor, it is raised in glory." I do not know what a glorified human body looks like, but I know it will be different from a body now. Earlier in 1 Corinthians 15, Paul wrote, "All flesh is not the same flesh, but there is one kind of flesh of men, another flesh of animals, another of fish, and another of birds. There are also celestial bodies and terrestrial bodies; but the glory of the celestial is one, and the glory of the terrestrial is another. There is one glory of the sun, another glory of the moon, and another glory of the stars; for one star differs from another star in glory" (vv. 39–41). Paul was simply saying that we see gradations, degrees of glory, all around us. What we have not yet seen is glorified humanity. But that was what came out of the tomb.

He went on: "It is sown in weakness, it is raised in power." The Bible extols the creative work that formed human beings. The psalmist said we are "fearfully and wonderfully made" (Ps. 139:14). Yet, the psalmist also prayed, "LORD, make me to know my end, and what is the measure of my days, that I may know how frail I am" (Ps. 39:4). When I reflect on my own life, I am sometimes surprised that this frail body could survive more than seven decades on this planet with all the diseases, maladies, and accidents that befall us. We are close to death every second, a heartbeat away, because our bodies are fundamentally weak. They do not have the capacity to sustain themselves indefinitely. Again, we are told, "The days of our lives are seventy years; and if by reason of strength they are eighty years, yet their boast is only labor and sorrow; for it is soon cut off, and we fly away" (Ps. 90:10). Truly we are sown in weakness, just as Jesus' body was put in the tomb in the weakness of human flesh. But the body that came out left that weakness behind. That body came out in power and in strength.

RAISED TO NEW HUMANITY

Paul declared:

> It is sown a natural body, it is raised a spiritual body.
> There is a natural body, and there is a spiritual body.

And so it is written, "The first man Adam became a living being." The last Adam became a life-giving spirit. However, the spiritual is not first, but the natural, and afterward the spiritual. The first man was of the earth, made of dust; the second Man is the Lord from heaven. As was the man of dust, so also are those who are made of dust; and as is the heavenly Man, so also are those who are heavenly. And as we have borne the image of the man of dust, we shall also bear the image of the heavenly Man. (1 Cor. 15:44–49)

Here is the crux of the work of Christ in the resurrection: He gives us a new humanity. He restores the original image of God in His people and prepares them to live forever.

Paul concluded by saying:

Now this I say, brethren, that flesh and blood cannot inherit the kingdom of God; nor does corruption inherit incorruption. Behold, I tell you a mystery: We shall not all sleep, but we shall all be changed— in a moment, in the twinkling of an eye, at the last trumpet. For the trumpet will sound, and the dead will be raised incorruptible, and we shall be changed. For this corruptible must put on incorruption, and this mortal must put on immortality. So when this corruptible has put on incorruption, and this mortal has put on immortality, then shall be brought to pass the saying that is written, "Death is swallowed up in victory." "O Death, where is your sting? O Hades, where is your victory?" The sting of death is sin, and the strength of sin is the law. But thanks be to God, who gives us the victory through the Lord Jesus Christ. (1 Cor. 15:50–57)

This is the point of the resurrection. The Father raised Jesus by the power of the Spirit, not simply for His own vindication, but for us. He was the first to be raised in this manner, being brought forth in a glorified state, but He will not be the last. Everyone who is in Christ Jesus will share in this resurrected glory. This is our hope. This hope is at the very heart and center of the Christian faith.

CHAPTER 10

STUDY GUIDE

INTRODUCTION

The Jewish and Roman leaders probably breathed a sigh of relief after Jesus died on the cross. They were finally rid of this man who had exposed their evil and hypocrisy. Or so they thought. In this chapter, Dr. R. C. Sproul looks at the redemptive significance of the resurrection of Jesus, explaining how it is at the very core of the Christian faith.

LEARNING OBJECTIVES

1. To be able to explain what it means to say that Jesus was raised for our justification.
2. To be able to explain why Paul would say that if Jesus was not raised our faith is in vain.

QUOTATIONS

> Rise, heart! thy Lord is risen. Sing his praise
> Without delays
> Who takes thee by the hand, that thou likewise
> With him mayst rise—
> That as his death calcined thee to dust,
> His life may make thee gold, and much more, just.
> —George Herbert, "Easter"

He alone has fully profited in the gospel who has accustomed himself to continual meditation upon the blessed resurrection.

—John Calvin, *Institutes of the Christian Religion*

OUTLINE

I. Introduction

    A. How can we speak of the resurrection as part of the work of Christ when it was an event in which He was completely passive?

    B. He was raised by the power of the Holy Spirit.

    C. Regarding the resurrection of Jesus, the first thing that must be observed is that He was really dead.

II. The Death of Death

    A. Paul described the resurrection of Jesus in connection with his discussion of the two Adams.

    B. The first Adam brought death into the world, while the second Adam brought resurrection from the dead.

    C. Death, the supreme enemy, was triumphed over in the resurrection.

    D. Here we see Christ as victor over Satan, sin, and death.

    E. He was not victorious over death only for Himself.

    F. God also raises up all who are in Christ.

    G. Believers participate in the triumph over death.

III. Raised by God

    A. When Lazarus was raised, he contributed nothing to it.

B. At the command of Jesus, he came to life.

C. The Holy Spirit raised Jesus to life.

D. It was impossible for Jesus to remain dead because death had no claim over Him.

IV. Raised for Our Justification

A. The New Testament tells us that Jesus was raised for our justification.

B. We know how the life and death of Christ relate to our justification, but what about His resurrection?

C. In the resurrection, the Father declared that He accepted the sacrifice of Christ.

V. The Resurrection Body

A. Paul taught that our bodies are sown in corruption but are raised incorruptible.

B. There was continuity between the body of Jesus before and after the resurrection, but there was also a dramatic change.

C. The body that came out of the tomb could never suffer decay.

D. We don't know exactly what a glorified body looks like, but we know it is different from what our bodies are now.

E. Christ gives us a new humanity.

F. Christ restores the image of God in His people and prepares them to live forever.

G. Everyone who is in Christ will share in His resurrection glory.

BIBLE STUDY

1. Read the following Old Testament texts. What glimpses of resurrection does each provide? Which texts seem to refer to individual resurrection, and which seem to speak of the national "resurrection" of Israel?

    a. Daniel 12:2–3
    b. Isaiah 26:19
    c. Hosea 6:1–2
    d. Ezekiel 37:1–14
    e. Job 19:23–27

2. The Apostle Paul discussed the resurrection of believers in many places. One of the more detailed passages is 1 Thessalonians 4:13–18. According to verses 16 and 17, what will occur when Christ returns?

3. One of the two key texts on the believer's resurrection is 2 Corinthians 4:7–5:10. How did Paul describe the present transformation of the Christian's inner nature in 4:7–18? How did he describe the future transformation of the Christian's body in 5:1–10?

4. The primary New Testament text on the resurrection is 1 Corinthians 15. Read this chapter and answer the following questions:

    a. What question was Paul responding to in this chapter according to verse 12?

    b. According to verses 13–19, what were the consequences of their denial of the resurrection of the dead?

    c. What is the order of resurrection according to verse 23?

    d. What is the eschatological significance of the resurrection according to verses 24–28?

    e. What is the difference between resurrection and the mere reanimation of a corpse according to verses 35–49?

    f. How is the resurrection tied to God's triumph over death according to verses 50–58?

DISCUSSION GUIDE

1. According to Paul, if Christ was not raised, the Christian faith is futile (1 Cor. 15:17–19). Why is the resurrection central to the Christian faith?

2. In 2 Timothy 2:16–19, we read of two men who were declaring that the resurrection had already happened. Since Jesus' resurrection had already happened, they were clearly referring to the resurrection of believers. Why did Paul condemn this teaching so strongly?

3. Having read 1 Corinthians 15, how would you describe the continuity and discontinuity between our present bodies and the bodies we will have at the resurrection?

APPLICATION

1. The hope of the resurrection causes Christians not to grieve at the death of believing loved ones the way unbelievers grieve. Give thanks to God that He has defeated death and that we will one day be reunited with believers who have gone to be with the Lord before us.

2. Read and meditate on Revelation 21:1–4. Consider what it will be like to live forever without death, mourning, crying, or pain.

SUGGESTED READING FOR FURTHER STUDY

Calvin, John. *Institutes of the Christian Religion*, 3.25.
Carson, D. A. *Scandalous: The Cross and Resurrection of Jesus*, pp. 112–68.
Davis, Stephen T. *Risen Indeed: Making Sense of the Resurrection*.
Hoekema, Anthony. *The Bible and the Future*, pp. 239–52.
Licona, Michael R. *The Resurrection of Jesus: A New Historiographical Approach*.

Mathison, Keith A. *From Age to Age.*

Ridderbos, Herman. *Paul: An Outline of His Theology*, pp. 537–51.

Strimple, Robert. "Hyper-Preterism on the Resurrection of the Body" in Keith Mathison, *When Shall These Things Be?*, pp. 287–352.

Venema, Cornelis. *The Promise of the Future*, pp. 363–91.

Vos, Geerhardus. *The Pauline Eschatology*, pp. 136–225.

11

ASCENSION

IF THERE IS ANY dimension of the life and the work of Jesus that is woefully neglected in the life of the church today, I believe it is His ascension. Yet, in New Testament categories, the ascension is the acme of Jesus' work.

In chapter 1, we saw that the incarnation was a descent; the second person of the Trinity came from heaven to earth in the body of a man. In that regard, I noted Paul's words to the Ephesians: "Therefore He says: 'When He ascended on high, He led captivity captive, and gave gifts to men.' (Now this, 'He ascended'—what does it mean but that He also first descended into the lower parts of the earth? He who descended is also the One who ascended far above all the heavens, that He might fill all things.)" (4:8–10). Paul's words at the end of this passage, "that He might fill all things," point to the reason Jesus ascended. So, the ascension was Jesus' return to heaven, but it was something far weightier than a return journey. It derives its significance from what Jesus went up to and for. Jesus' ministry culminated with His ascension to heaven for His coronation as Lord of all things.

Luke gave us two accounts of the ascension, one at the end of his gospel and one in the opening chapter of the book of Acts. He wrote:

> And He led them out as far as Bethany, and He lifted up His hands and blessed them. Now it came to pass, while He blessed them, that He was parted from them and carried up into heaven. And they worshiped Him, and returned to Jerusalem with great joy, and were continually in the temple praising and blessing God. Amen. (Luke 24:50–53)

> Now when He had spoken these things, while they watched, He was taken up, and a cloud received Him out of their sight. And while they looked steadfastly toward heaven as He went up, behold, two men stood by them in white apparel, who also said, "Men of Galilee, why do you stand gazing up into heaven? This same Jesus, who was taken up from you into heaven, will so come in like manner as you saw Him go into heaven." (Acts 1:9–11)

In Luke's first account, we simply read that Jesus was taken up; he said nothing about how Jesus was taken up. In the Acts version, Luke told us that Jesus basically was taken up in a cloud, which is significant, because that would be the *shekinah* cloud, the cloud that manifests the glory of God throughout the Scriptures.

A DIFFERENT REACTION

The reaction of the disciples is interesting. In his gospel, Luke told us that after Jesus was lifted up, the disciples returned to Jerusalem with great joy, and they were constantly praising God. This is fascinating to me because, when Jesus first told the disciples that He was departing, there was no sense of joy whatsoever. Here is John's account:

> "A little while, and you will not see Me; and again a little while, and you will see Me, because I go to the Father." Then some of His disciples said among themselves, "What is this that He says to us, 'A little while, and you will not see Me; and again a little while, and you will see Me'; and, 'because I go to the Father'?" They said therefore, "What is this that He says, 'A little while'? We do not know what He is saying." Now Jesus knew that they desired to ask Him, and He said to them, "Are you inquiring among

yourselves about what I said, 'A little while, and you will not see Me; and again a little while, and you will see Me'? Most assuredly, I say to you that you will weep and lament, but the world will rejoice; and you will be sorrowful, but your sorrow will be turned into joy." (16:16–20)

The worst thing that Jesus could have told His disciples at that point—from the disciples' point of view—was that He was leaving them. They did not want Him ever to leave. They could not imagine how His departure would be of any redemptive value whatsoever. He had explained to them that it was to their advantage that He depart (John 16:7), but they did not understand it. In many ways, I think, the church still has not understood it. Many believers, exercising their proclivity for nostalgia, wish they could have been alive during the earthly sojourn of Jesus. Yet, we should understand that His absence from this earth is better for us right now than His presence was during the first century.

Somewhere between Jesus' explanation to His disciples that it would be an advantage for them if He departed and His actual departure, their feelings changed from deep sorrow and disappointment to great joy. Why? Were they happy to see Him go? Of course not. But they came to understand why He went and where He was going, and that was the cause of their joy.

I believe we, too, can appreciate and rejoice in the ascension of Jesus if we understand four results of it.

THE GLORIFICATION OF CHRIST

First, the ascension restored Jesus' glory. In His High Priestly Prayer in the upper room on the night before He died, Jesus prayed:

> Father, the hour has come. Glorify Your Son, that Your Son also may glorify You, as You have given Him authority over all flesh, that He should give eternal life to as many as You have given Him. And this is eternal life, that they may know You, the only true God, and Jesus Christ whom You have sent. I have glorified You on the earth. I have finished the work which You have given Me to do. And now, O Father, glorify Me together with Yourself, with the glory which I had with You before the world was. (John 17:1–5)

Jesus left His glory when He descended in the incarnation. Here He prayed in the upper room: "Father, let Me have My glory back. Let Me enjoy the glory I had with You from the foundation of the world." When Jesus departed this world on the *shekinah* cloud, He was going back to the realm of glory. He was going to receive the glory that He enjoyed with the Father from all eternity. So, the ascension was a glorious thing. That is why, after He ascended, the disciples went back into Jerusalem and praised God in the temple. They understood that their Master was getting His glory back. His humiliation was over, and His exaltation had begun.

THE CORONATION OF THE KING

Second, in the ascension, Jesus went up to His coronation. He did not go up simply to enter into His rest. He went up for His investiture service. He ascended to the throne, to the right hand of God, where He was given dominion, power, and authority over the whole earth. The Lamb who was slain became the Lion of Judah, who now reigns over the earth.

Again, the church has failed to understand. Many still look at the kingdom of God as something in the unfulfilled future. But the kingdom has begun. Why? Because the King has been enthroned. When we recite the Apostles' Creed, we affirm that Jesus "ascended into heaven and sitteth at the right hand of God the Father Almighty." He now sits in the seat of authority at the right hand of the Father, acting, as it were, as the celestial Prime Minister. The New Testament gives Him the titles of King of Kings and Lord of Lords (1 Tim. 6:15; Rev. 17:14; 19:16). Jesus is no longer a peripatetic rabbi, walking around Galilee and Judea. He is enthroned, and no monarch in this world can rule for a second apart from His authority. He brings kingdoms up and brings kingdoms down. He is accountable to no earthly ruler.

Needless to say, the reign of our Lord is a tremendous benefit for those who love Him and follow Him. For this reason, it is clearly better for us that Jesus left than if He had stayed.

THE GIFT OF THE COMFORTER

Third, the ascension set the stage for Pentecost. Also in the upper room on the night before His death, Jesus explained that He was going away in order that He might send His disciples "another Helper" (John 14:16), the Holy Spirit. The Greek word translated as "Helper" here is *Parakletos,* from which we get the English word *paraclete,* which we often use as a synonym for the Holy Spirit. However, the Holy Spirit is not *the* Paraclete; He is *another* Paraclete. The original Paraclete was Christ Himself.

The Old English translations of *Parakletos* often render it as "Comforter." When we read the word *comforter,* we think of one who brings consolation to those who are in pain and suffering. However, we need to understand the word *comforter* as it was used in Old English, when it meant "with strength." It was not so much solace that was in view in the ministry of the Spirit as it was power and strength.

The word *parakletos* literally means "one called alongside." In the ancient world, the parakletos was the family attorney. If a person was facing a difficult problem, he would summon the parakletos, and the parakletos would come alongside the person and help him through his problem.

Jesus told the disciples they were going to have problems: "They will put you out of the synagogues; yes, the time is coming that whoever kills you will think that he offers God service" (John 16:2). For this reason, He gave them the promise of the Holy Spirit, a *Parakletos,* to give them strength, to stand beside them in times of crisis so that they might prove faithful. This is why He told them, "Tarry in the city of Jerusalem until you are endued with power from on high" (Luke 24:49).

The last question the disciples asked Jesus before the ascension was this: "Lord, will You at this time restore the kingdom to Israel?" Jesus replied: "It is not for you to know times or seasons which the Father has put in His own authority. But you shall receive power when the Holy Spirit has come upon you; and you shall be witnesses to Me in Jerusalem, and in all Judea and Samaria, and to the end of the earth" (Acts 1:6–8). So, one of the most important reasons for Jesus' ascension was that Pentecost might take place, that the Father and the Son might pour out the Spirit on the church to strengthen it and empower it for its earthly mission. As we all know, to witness for Christ in a corrupt world requires strength greater than our own. John Calvin said that the most important task of the church is to be the visible witness of the invisible kingdom, and for that we need the Holy Spirit.

THE MINISTRY OF THE HIGH PRIEST

Fourth, the ascension inaugurated Jesus' ministry as our High Priest. The author of Hebrews wrote, "Christ came as High Priest of the good things to come, with the greater and more perfect tabernacle not made with hands, that is, not of this creation. Not with the blood of goats and calves, but with His own blood He entered the Most Holy Place once for all, having obtained eternal redemption" (9:11–12). We have a great High Priest who offered a sacrifice for us on the cross once and for all—His own blood. That portion of His priestly ministry is finished. But His priestly work for us goes on as He intercedes for us. On the night before He died, Jesus prayed:

> I have manifested Your name to the men whom you have given Me out of the world. They were Yours, You gave them to Me, and they have kept Your word. Now they have known that all things which You have given Me are from You. For I have given to them the words which You have given Me; and they have received them, and have known surely that I came forth from You; and they have believed that You sent Me. I pray for them. I do not pray for the world but for those whom You have given Me, for they are Yours. And all Mine are Yours, and Yours are Mine, and I am glorified in them. Now I am no longer in the world, but these are in the world, and I come to You. Holy Father, keep through Your name those whom You have given Me, that they may be one as We are. (John 17:6–11)

We have a doctrine called the perseverance of the saints. I do not like that name for it; while saints do persevere, it is not because they have the power of perseverance within themselves. If it were left to me to persevere in my Christian walk, I would fall and stumble in a moment. The One who really perseveres is God.

He perseveres with His children and thereby preserves them. One of the chief ways in which God preserves His people is through the priestly intercession of Jesus.

We see an example of this from the night when Jesus was betrayed. When Jesus and His disciples gathered in the upper room, He announced to them that one of them was going to betray Him, speaking of Judas. The disciples were perplexed, wondering which of them it might be. Finally, Jesus identified Judas by handing him a piece of bread and saying, "What you do, do quickly" (John 13:21–27). After that, Jesus dismissed Judas to carry out his treachery.

However, there was another disciple at the table who was going to deny Jesus that night. So Jesus said to him: "Simon, Simon! Indeed, Satan has asked for you, that he may sift you as wheat. But I have prayed for you, that your faith should not fail; and when you have returned to Me, strengthen your brethren" (Luke 22:31–32).

What was the difference between Judas and Peter? Jesus did not pray for Judas. He said, "While I was with them in the world, I kept them in Your name. Those whom You gave Me I have kept; and none of them is lost except the son of perdition" (John 17:12). Peter was one whom the Father had given to Jesus. His denial was a ghastly and heinous crime, but Jesus had prayed for him, and He commanded Peter to strengthen his brothers when he returned. Not *if* he returned, but *when*. So, the prayer of Jesus for Peter was effective.

Today, Jesus is in heaven, interceding for you and me, if indeed we belong to Him, and His prayers for us are equally effective. We should rejoice that He has taken up this priestly ministry on our behalf in the heavenly tabernacle.

CHAPTER 11

STUDY GUIDE

INTRODUCTION

Christians spend a great deal of time thinking about the birth, death, resurrection, and second coming of Jesus, but the ascension of Christ is often overlooked. Yet the ascension was the event that marked Christ's enthronement, His return to glory. In this chapter, Dr. R. C. Sproul explains why the ascension of Christ is so significant.

LEARNING OBJECTIVES

1. To understand the place of the ascension in redemptive history.
2. To be able to explain four important things that occurred because of the ascension of Christ.

QUOTATIONS

> Faith has in its foundation four great corner-stones on which the building rests—the Divinity of Christ, the Incarnation, the Atonement on the Cross, the Ascension to the Throne. The last is the most wonderful, the crown of all the rest, the perfect revelation of what God has made Christ for us. And so in the Christian life it is the most important, the glorious fruit of all that goes before.
>
> —Andrew Murray, *The Holiest of All*

> The Ascension and Ascended Life bear witness against the materialistic spirit which threatens in some quarters to overpower those higher interests that have their seat in the region of the spiritual and eternal. They are as a *Sursum corda*—"lift up your hearts"—which comes down from the High Priest of the Church who stands at the heavenly altar, and draws forth from the kneeling Church the answer *Habemus ad*

Dominum—"we lift them up unto the Lord."

—H. B. Swete, *The Ascended Christ*

OUTLINE

I. Introduction

    A. If there is any dimension of the life and work of Christ that is neglected in the church today, it is His ascension.

    B. The ascension was Christ's return to heaven after completing His atoning work.

II. The Ascension

    A. Luke gave us a record of the ascension in two places: at the end of his gospel and in the first chapter of Acts.

    B. In the gospel account, Luke told us that after the ascension, the disciples returned to Jerusalem with great joy.

    C. They were not happy that Jesus was gone, but they understood where He went and why, and that was the cause for their joy.

    D. Four things occurred because of the ascension of Christ, and these four things are the reason why it was to our advantage that Jesus departed.

III. Exaltation to Glory

A. In John 17, Jesus spoke of the glory He had with the Father before the world was created and looked forward to enjoying it again.

B. At the ascension, Jesus returned to the realm of glory.

C. His time of humiliation was over, and He was being exalted.

IV. The Coronation of the King

A. A second thing that occurred at the ascension was Christ's coronation.

B. Jesus was brought up to the right hand of the Father, where He was given all authority.

C. The kingdom of God is not something away in the future.

D. The kingdom has begun because the King has been enthroned.

E. Jesus is now the King of Kings and Lord of Lords.

V. Pentecost

A. Jesus also explained to His disciples that He was going away in order that He might send them another Paraclete.

B. The original Paraclete was Jesus; the Holy Spirit is *another* Paraclete.

C. The paraclete was the name given to the family attorney in the ancient world.

D. *Parakletos* is one called to stand alongside of you.

E. Jesus sent the Paraclete to give His people strength.

F. One of the most important reasons for Jesus' ascension was that Pentecost might take place.

G. At Pentecost, the Holy Spirit was poured out on the church in order to empower it for its earthly mission.

VI. The Intercession of the High Priest

A. The fourth thing that happened at the ascension was that Jesus as our High Priest entered into the heavenly Holy of Holies, where He functions as our Priest-King.

B. His chief priestly work now is the work of intercession.

C. He is not making sacrifices in heaven.

D. Jesus prays for those who have been given to Him.

E. He prays for our perseverance.

BIBLE STUDY

1. Read Acts 1:6–8. What were the last words spoken by Jesus before His ascension? What promise did He make to His disciples? What was His final commission to them? Did His final commission answer the disciples' original question in verse 6?

2. Read Acts 1:9–11.

    a. Compare these verses with Daniel 7:13–14. What similarities do you detect? In light of Acts 2:22–36, is Christ's ascension the fulfillment of Daniel's prophecy?

    b. How did Luke emphasize the visibility of the ascension in verses 9–11?

    c. How does the appearance of the two men compare to the events recorded in Luke 9:30 and Luke 24:4?

3. The book of Hebrews tells us about Jesus' ministry as our great High Priest. What do the following texts add to our understanding of this ministry?

    a. Hebrews 4:14–16

    b. Hebrews 5:9

    c. Hebrews 7:23–28

    d. Hebrews 8:1–13

    e. Hebrews 9:11–14

    f. Hebrews 9:23–28

    g. Hebrews 10:11–14

DISCUSSION GUIDE

1. Many commentators argue that Daniel 7:13–14 is a prophecy of Christ's second coming. John Calvin, on the other hand, argued

that it was a prophecy of Christ's ascension. Comparing Daniel 7:13–14 with Acts 1:9–11 (the account of the ascension) and with 1 Thessalonians 4:16 (a New Testament prophecy of the second coming), which interpretation of Daniel 7 is strongest? Why?

2. H. B. Swete said, "The Ascension and Ascended Life bear witness against the materialistic spirit which threatens in some quarters to overpower those higher interests that have their seat in the region of the spiritual and eternal."[1] Is this true? If so, how does a proper understanding of these doctrines guard against a materialistic/worldly spirit?

3. Liberals and skeptics repeatedly claim that the traditional interpretation of Acts 1:9–11 necessitates the adoption of a false three-tiered understanding of the universe as well as the idea that heaven is located at some physical point somewhere in space. This objection is frequently raised in the writings of men such as Rudolf Bultmann and John Shelby Spong. But does a traditional interpretation of Acts 1:9–11 require us to believe that heaven is located somewhere in the sky above the clouds? Is heaven a different spiritual dimension of existence? If so, what reasons, didactic or otherwise, might Jesus have had for visibly ascending some distance before entering the heavenly dimension of existence?

APPLICATION

1. Read the words of the two men to the disciples in Acts 1:11. Consider what this means in terms of where you should focus your attention each day.

2. Take time today to meditate on the fact that Christ was exalted at the ascension as both King and High Priest, and on what this means for you as a believer in Jesus.

SUGGESTED READING FOR FURTHER STUDY

Bavinck, Herman. *Reformed Dogmatics,* vol. 3, pp. 442–47.
Bunyan, John. *The Intercession of Christ.*
Calvin, John. *Institutes of the Christian Religion,* 2.16.14–16.
Dawson, Gerrit Scott. *Jesus Ascended.*
Metzger, Bruce. *Historical and Literary Studies,* pp. 77–87.
Swete, H. B. *The Ascended Christ.*
Witsius, Herman. *Sacred Dissertations on the Apostles' Creed,* vol. 2, pp. 198–236.

NOTES: CHAPTER 11

1. H. B. Swete, *The Ascended Christ: A Study in the Earliest Christian Teaching* (London: Macmillan, 1910), 155.

12

RETURN

EVEN THOUGH JESUS COMPLETED His earthly work when He died on the cross and rose again, and He has ascended into heaven, where He sits at the right hand of the Father, He has more yet to do. He will come again at the end of time to finish the work of His kingdom.

For centuries, the church has referred to the return of Jesus as the Blessed Hope. The return of Jesus certainly is our hope. It is something we long to see, an event we cannot wait to experience. Unfortunately, when we use the word *hope* in the English language, we refer to something that we wish would happen, not something that is guaranteed to come to pass. If you were to ask me whether I think the Pittsburgh Steelers will win the Super Bowl this season, I would say, "I hope so, but I'm not sure." I simply cannot be sure that the Steelers will win another championship this season. However, in New Testament categories, the Greek word *elpis,* which is translated as "hope," does not lack certainty. The hope of which the New Testament speaks refers to the promises God has made, the fulfillment of which is absolutely certain. There is no doubt about it. So, the Blessed Hope is really our Blessed Assurance. We can rest assured that Jesus will return someday.

The New Testament has a lot to say about Jesus' future return. One passage that addresses it is in Paul's first letter to the Thessalonians, where he wrote:

> But I do not want you to be ignorant, brethren, concerning those who have fallen asleep, lest you sorrow as others who have no hope. For if we believe that Jesus died and rose again, even so God will bring with Him those who sleep in Jesus. For this we say to you by the word of the Lord, that we who are alive and remain until the coming of the Lord will by no means precede those who are asleep. For the Lord Himself will descend from heaven with a shout, with the voice of an archangel, and with the trumpet of God. And the dead in Christ will rise first. Then we who are alive and remain shall be caught up together with them in the clouds to meet the Lord in the air. And thus we shall always be with the Lord. Therefore, comfort one another with these words. (4:13–18)

This is Paul's teaching about what is popularly called the rapture. The rapture is the miraculous transportation of all living Christians to heaven at the return of Jesus. There is a lot of misinformation about this event, but this passage gives us some definite truths about it. Paul made it clear that Jesus' return will not be secret but will be visible; it will be a bodily return; and it will be a triumphant return, for He will not come in lowliness and meekness as He did at His first advent, but in power and glory. As we saw in the previous chapter, the angels told the disciples, "This same Jesus, who was taken up from you into heaven, will so come in like manner as you saw Him go into heaven" (Acts 1:11). Just as He left visibly on the *shekinah* cloud, so He will come again visibly on this cloud of glory.

There is a view, one that is very widespread in the church today, that holds that Jesus will come back to rapture the church out of the world, but that the great tribulation will then occur, after which Jesus will return again. I think this view is a result of a serious misunderstanding of what the Apostle described here in 1 Thessalonians.

I once spoke with one of the leading representatives of this school of thought, a man who teaches the "pretribulation" rapture. I said to him, "I do not know a single verse anywhere in the Bible that teaches a pretribulation rapture. Can you tell me where to find that?" I'll never forget what he said to me: "No, I can't. But that's what I was taught from the time I was a little child." I told him, "Let's get our theology from the Bible rather than from Sunday school lessons we heard years and years ago."

PARTICIPATING IN CHRIST'S RETURN

Let us look at the events Paul described. First he noted: "The Lord Himself will descend from heaven.… And the dead in Christ will rise first. Then we who are alive and remain shall be caught up together with them in the clouds to meet the Lord in the air" (1 Thess. 4:16–17). Here we see that the purpose of the dead rising and our being caught up into the sky is not to go away but to meet Jesus as He is returning. He will not be taking us out of the world to stay. He will be lifting us up to participate with Him in His triumphal return.

When the Roman legions were dispatched to go into a foreign country on a military campaign, their standards bore the letters SPQR, an abbreviation for *Senatus Populus Que Romanus*, which means "the Senate and the people of Rome." It was understood in Rome that the conquests of the military were not simply for the politicians who governed, but for all the citizens of the city.

The army might be gone for a campaign of two or three years. Finally, the soldiers would return, leading captives in chains. They would camp outside the city and send in a messenger to alert the Senate and the people that the legions had returned. When that news arrived, the people began to prepare to receive the conquering heroes. When everything was ready, a trumpet was sounded. With that, the citizens of the city went out to where the army was camped and joined the soldiers in marching into the city. The idea was that they had participated in the triumph of their conquering army.

This is exactly the language that Paul used here. He was saying that when Jesus comes back in conquering power, believers, both dead and alive, will be caught up in the air to meet Him, not to stay up there, but to join His return in triumph, to participate in His exaltation.

It seems that Paul's goal here was to comfort the Thessalonians, who were saddened that their dead loved ones were apparently going to miss the triumphal return of Christ, the great conclusion to the ministry of Jesus at the end of time. Paul assured them that the dead in Christ will not miss His return at all. In fact, they will be there first. The dead will rise first, and then those who are still alive and are Christ's will be caught up together with this whole assembly to come to the earth again in triumph.

AN UPSURGE OF APOSTASY

In his second letter to the Thessalonians, Paul had to correct some misunderstandings about the return of Christ. He wrote:

> Now, brethren, concerning the coming of our Lord Jesus Christ and our gathering together to Him, we ask you, not to be soon shaken in mind or troubled, either by spirit or by word or by letter, as if from us, as though the day of Christ had come. Let no one deceive you by any means; for that Day will not come unless the falling away comes first, and the man

of sin is revealed, the son of perdition, who opposes and exalts himself above all that is called God or that is worshiped, so that he sits as God in the temple of God, showing himself that he is God.

Do you not remember that when I was still with you I told you these things? And now you know what is restraining, that he may be revealed in his own time. For the mystery of lawlessness is already at work; only He who now restrains will do so until He is taken out of the way. And then the lawless one will be revealed, whom the Lord will consume with the breath of His mouth and destroy with the brightness of His coming. The coming of the lawless one is according to the working of Satan, with all power, signs, and lying wonders, and with all unrighteous deception among those who perish, because they did not receive the love of the truth, that they might be saved. And for this reason God will send them strong delusion, that they should believe the lie, that they all may be condemned who did not believe the truth but had pleasure in unrighteousness. (2:1–12)

Paul was saying that before Christ returns, there will be the great apostasy. Apostasy is not the same as paganism. Pagans are people who have never professed faith in Christ. Apostates are people who have made a profession of faith in Christ, but who have fallen away from the truth of the gospel. Churches can become apostate, going from a confession of faith that is godly, biblical, and true to an embrace of pagan concepts and behavioral patterns. When a church repudiates its confession in this way, it is not a valid church anymore. It is apostate. Likewise, people in the visible church who have made a public profession of faith, only to deny it later, are apostate. (Of course, this cannot happen to true believers, those who have made a true profession of faith and actually possess the faith they profess, for God preserves them from falling away from Him.)

Apostasy happens in some measure in every age. But Paul described a great apostasy. He told us that around the time Jesus is about to come back, we can expect widespread apostasy in the church. Many people are convinced that the final advent of Christ is close because of the widespread manifestations of apostasy that we see today in the mainline churches in the United States, in Europe, and around the world.

THE APPEARANCE OF THE ANTICHRIST

Paul also told us that the "man of sin … the son of perdition, who opposes and exalts himself above all that is called God or that is worshiped," must be revealed before Christ returns. Here he was describing what we normally refer to as the Antichrist. In our language, *anti* means "to be opposed to or to be against." However, the New Testament idea of the Antichrist refers to someone who is more than simply against Christ. In the Greek, *anti* means "against and a substitute for," so the Antichrist will not be merely an opponent of Christ; he will be one who seeks to usurp the office of Christ and to substitute himself for Christ. He will set himself up in the temple as if he were God. That is why it is usually thought that the Antichrist will be someone who is in the religious realm, someone who disguises himself as a good person but is actually working to undermine the authority of Jesus, just as Satan disguises himself as an angel of light (2 Cor. 11:14).

Paul went on to say, "The mystery of lawlessness is already at work" (2 Thess. 2:7). In his first epistle, the Apostle John wrote, "Little children, it is the last hour; and as you have heard that the Antichrist is coming, even now many antichrists have come, by which we know that it is the last hour" (1 John 2:18). So, there will be a multitude of antichrists leading up to the Antichrist, the supreme or worst antichrist, who comes at the end. He will come using deceptive powers, working with the powers of Satan, in order to convince people of falsehood rather than the truth. However, we are told that he will be destroyed. The Lord Jesus "will consume [him] with the breath of His mouth and destroy [him] with the brightness of His coming" (2 Thess. 2:8).

So, we do not look for the second advent of Jesus to appear until after a great apostasy and a tribulation brought about by the Antichrist, because it will be while the Antichrist is here that Christ will come and destroy him.

That is our hope, and it cannot fail to be fulfilled.

CHAPTER 12

STUDY GUIDE

INTRODUCTION

At the ascension of Christ, the disciples were promised that Jesus would come again, and the second coming of Christ has remained the church's Blessed Hope ever since. The second coming has also been the source of great controversy. In this chapter, Dr. R. C. Sproul explains some of the basic facts concerning the second coming, while at the same time dispelling some common misconceptions.

LEARNING OBJECTIVES

1. To be able to explain the nature of Christ's second coming.
2. To be able to explain the nature of the apostasy that will precede the second coming.

QUOTATIONS

All sorrow which we might conceive, because of Christ's absence, is mitigated, yea, utterly taken away, when as we hear that he shall return again.

—John Calvin, *Commentary upon the Acts of the Apostles*

When we think of the way in which Christ, having renewed our souls, is going to renew our bodies so that they will be like his glorious body, how he will receive us when we go forth to meet him in the air, how he will vindicate us in the final judgment, how we shall dwell with him forever in a gloriously renewed universe; and when, in addition to all this, we reflect on the fact that we had deserved none of this glory but only everlasting damnation, then, indeed, we by his grace will prepare ourselves thoroughly to meet him at his coming!

—William Hendriksen, *The Bible on the Life Hereafter*

OUTLINE

I. Introduction

    A. The return of Christ at the end of time will mark the consummation of His kingdom.

    B. For centuries the church has referred to the return of Jesus as the Blessed Hope.

    C. In the New Testament, "hope" refers to those promises the fulfillment of which is absolutely certain.

II. The Rapture

    A. In 1 Thessalonians 4:13–18, Paul spoke of the second coming and of what is called "the rapture."

    B. The rapture refers to believers being caught up in the air at Christ's return.

    C. Jesus' second coming will be visible, bodily, and triumphant.

    D. Acts 1:11 teaches that He will come just as He went—visibly and bodily.

    E. The popular dispensationalist view known as "pretribulationism" is based on a serious misunderstanding of Paul's teaching.

III. Triumphal Return

A. The purpose of the dead rising and the living being caught up together is not to go away, but to meet Jesus as He is returning.

B. Jesus lifts us up to participate in His triumphal return.

C. In ancient times, when a conquering king returned to Rome, the populace would go out to meet him and accompany him back into the city.

D. The Thessalonians were worried that those who had died would miss out, but Paul assured them that the dead will get to go first.

IV. Great Apostasy

A. In 2 Thessalonians 2, Paul corrected some misunderstandings about Christ's coming.

B. He told the Thessalonians some things that must take place before Christ comes again.

C. Before Christ comes there will be a great apostasy.

D. Apostasy refers to those who have made a profession of faith falling away from the truth of the gospel.

E. This cannot happen to true believers, but only to those who have made a false profession.

V. The Antichrist

A. Paul also added that the man of sin must be revealed.

B. Paul was describing what we usually call the Antichrist.

C. The Antichrist is not merely an opponent of God; he actually seeks to usurp Christ's office and to substitute himself for God.

D. It is usually thought that the Antichrist will be someone in the religious realm.

E. There are multitudes of lowercase *a* antichrists.

F. These all lead up to the culmination in the capital *A* Antichrist, who comes at the end.

G. Christ will destroy the Antichrist at His coming.

H. We don't look for the second coming of Christ until after the apostasy and after the coming of the Antichrist.

BIBLE STUDY

1. Read Acts 1:11. What can we learn about the nature of Christ's second coming from this text?

2. Paul described several events in connection with the second coming in 1 Thessalonians 4:13–18. In verse 14, Paul comforted the Thessalonians by telling them that Jesus will bring with Him those who have fallen asleep (i.e., died). How will Jesus do that according to verse 16?

3. How does 1 Corinthians 15:51–52 contribute to our understanding of what happens at the second coming?

DISCUSSION GUIDE

1. Many Christians from the earliest centuries of the church to this day have thought they could calculate the timing of the second coming of Christ. Is this possible? Why or why not? What kind of damage can be (and has been) done by well-meaning date setters?

2. Do most Christians in your circle of experience live and behave as if they really believe that Jesus will return? What general examples can you provide to substantiate your answer?

3. The church has always confessed its belief in the future second coming of Christ, general resurrection, and final judgment. These doctrines are incorporated into every orthodox creed and confession. Should a particular view of the end times be placed on the same level as determinative of orthodoxy and fellowship? Why or why not?

APPLICATION

1. Consider what you can do to increase in your heart and the hearts of others a joyful longing and expectation of the return of Jesus.

2. If Jesus were to return right now, would you be ashamed? What do you need to do in order not to be ashamed?

SUGGESTED READING FOR FURTHER STUDY

Bavinck, Herman. *Reformed Dogmatics,* vol. 4, pp. 684–90.

Hodge, Charles. *Systematic Theology,* vol. 3, pp. 790–800.

Hoekema, Anthony. *The Bible and the Future,* pp. 109–28.

Mathison, Keith A. *From Age to Age,* pp. 463–66, 511–14.

Poythress, Vern S. *Understanding Dispensationalists.*

Venema, Cornelis P. *The Promise of the Future,* pp. 79–109.

Vos, Geerhardus. *The Pauline Eschatology,* pp. 72–135.

ABOUT THE AUTHOR

Dr. R. C. Sproul is the founder and chairman of Ligonier Ministries, an international Christian education ministry based near Orlando, Florida. He also serves as senior minister of preaching and teaching at Saint Andrew's, a Reformed congregation in Sanford, Florida, and as president of Reformation Bible College. His teaching can be heard on the daily radio program *Renewing Your Mind*.

During his distinguished academic career, Dr. Sproul helped train men for the ministry as a professor at several leading theological seminaries.

He is the author of more than seventy books, including *The Holiness of God, Chosen by God, The Invisible Hand, Faith Alone, Truths We Confess, The Truth of the Cross,* and *The Prayer of the Lord.*

He also served as general editor of *The Reformation Study Bible* and has written several children's books, including *The Prince's Poison Cup*.

Dr. Sproul and his wife, Vesta, make their home in Longwood, Florida.

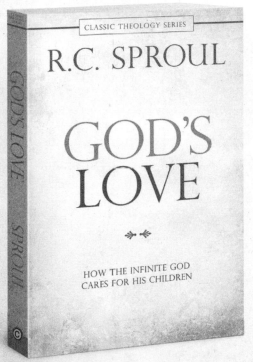

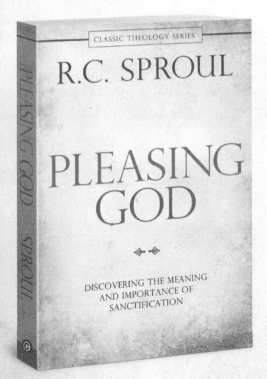